FLYING THE

BIG BIRDS

ON BECOMING AN AIRLINE PILOT

FLYING THE

BIG BIRDS

ON BECOMING AN AIRLINE PILOT

By Sylvia J. Otypka

Leading Edge Publishing
PO Box 461605
Aurora, CO 80046-1605

I have done my best to give you useful and accurate information on becoming an airline pilot. The data in this book is currant as of the copyright date. Please be aware that laws, regulations, and procedures are constantly changing and are subject to differing interpretations. You have the responsibility to check all material you read here before relying on it. Of necessity, I do not render specific legal or professional services or make any warranties concerning the information in this book or the use to which it is put.

Every effort has been made to seek approval and confer recognition to the source of the data used prior to publication. If notified, the publisher will be pleased to rectify any omission in the next edition of this book.

First Printing January 1997

Cover photo provided courtesy of United Airlines.

The photo of Marilyn Koon and the photo of the Air Force Academy was contributed by Kelly Hamilton. Emily Howell Warner contributed the photo of herself. All other photos were taken by the author.

Illustrations by Lenn Richter, 13699 Sidney Road SW, Port Orchard, WA 98366.

Printing by Book Masters, Inc., 2541 Ashland Road, PO Box 2139, Mansfield, OH 44905.

Attention organizations, universities, and schools:
Quantity discounts are available on bulk purchases of this book for educational purposes. Special books or book excerpts can also be created to fit specific needs. For information please contact Leading Edge Publishing, PO Box 461605, Aurora, CO 80046-1605.

ACKNOWLEDGMENTS

I would like to send very special thanks to Steve Barnhardt and Cindy Brody for their continual support and belief in me throughout all my endeavors.

Additionally I would like to thank Colonel Kelly Hamilton, USAF, for the plethora of information she imparted to me on the Military. Thanks also go to Sally Fodie and Jean Harper for their encouragement and assistance. Special appreciation goes to Henry M. Holden for his publishing expertise and motivational support. A warm thanks to Lenn Richter for his quick and professional work on the illustrations. I would also like to thank Steve Barnhardt and Pat Ponczek for editing the book and deeming it fit for human consumption.

Appreciation also goes to the following people for their contributions: Jim Attley, PARC; Peggy Baty, WAI; John Bauserman, UAL; CDR Trish Beckman, USN, WMA; Cheryl Cage, Cage Consulting; Amy Carmien, WAI; Lori Cline, ISA; Joe Coates, UAL; Kit Darby, Air Inc.; Mario Ecung, OBAP; Bill Evans, Aviation Explorer Scouts; Carol Janni, UAL; Karen Kahn, Aviation Career Counseling; Chet Kollett, UAL; Marilyn Koon, ISA; Betsy Landon, ISA; Bob Lund, Pilot; Kathleen Malone, ISA; Mary Mason, CAP; Luan Meredith, ISA; David NewMyer, SIU; Carolyn Pasqualino, ISA; Gayle Schimpf, UAL Media; July Tarver, UPAS; Jean Tinsley, Whirly-Girls; Denise Van Grunsven, ISA; Emily Howell Warner, FAA; Susan White, UAL Employment; Carolyn Williamson, UAA; and Krisan Wismer, ISA; Annette Worthington, ISA.

I would like to thank all the pilots, United Airlines flight crews, and the Colorado Air National Guard for allowing me to photograph them in action.

My appreciation to anyone whom I have inadvertently neglected to mention, you know what part you have added and I thank you for it.

HERE'S WHAT PEOPLE ARE SAYING ABOUT
Flying The Big Birds:

"Flying The Big Birds is an excellent, informative guide for anyone aspiring to a career in aviation. The author knows her subject and has provided a concise overview of available options. The list of resources will be helpful as you pursue your goals. Aviation can be a rewarding and challenging career. Aim high and make your dream a reality!"

Dr. David R. Williams
Astronaut
Commercial pilot
Married to an airline pilot

"Flying The Big Birds is an important contribution to aviation literature. It provides abundant resources and reference materials for anyone thinking of becoming an airline pilot. Writing from her personal experience, Otypka provides a well balanced and thought out plan that can make a positive difference for the reader's journey to the cockpit of the Big Birds."

Henry M. Holden
Author of eight aviation books
Historian, Pilot, Publisher, & Speaker

"Flying The Big Birds is a well thought out plan of attack for any aspiring pilot! It is helpful to see both the military and the civilian routes mapped out side by side explaining all the options. I especially appreciate the honest look at women and their unique experiences in this career."

Ms. Andrea Mesec
Student Pilot
Author
School Teacher

"I am happy to see a book such as this finally hit the market. There are not enough books like *Flying The Big Birds* which provide useful advice about how to enter the aviation field. What I like most about the book is its readability and its practicality for young adults. This book will provide a helpful foundation for any beginning pilot, as well as excellent resource material for pilots with a few ratings and questions about what to do next. As Ms. Otypka notes, it is a worthy goal indeed to find a career where in you get paid to have this much fun. Happy aviating!"

Dr. David A. NewMyer
Department Chair
Aviation Management & Flight
Southern Illinois University at Carbondale

"A *must have* reference and source document for all libraries and career counselors. This book is an essential primer and consolidation of sources on *how to get there from here* for any aviator. An especially informative book for female aviation aspirants. Anyone seeking to be a military pilot can find all the essential source information in this book. Consider the Service Academies where you can serve your nation while gaining government provided flight instruction, aviation experience, and a university degree."

Joe Coates
United Airlines Boeing 747-400 pilot
Former Vice Commandant of Cadets, USAF Academy
Retired USAF Colonel

"*Flying The Big Birds* was a real joy for me to read. It was very accurate and informative. As a board member, I will recommend this book to the International Women in Aerospace Museum to be included in the collections on Women Airline Pilots."

Captain Emily Howell Warner
First Women Pilot hired by a US Air Carrier, 1973
FAA Aircrew Program Manager

TABLE OF CONTENTS

ABOUT THE AUTHOR

Sylvia Otypka (O·Tip·ka) is a pilot for United Airlines with over 11,000 hours of flight time. She has been working for United since 1985, flying the Boeing 727, 757, 767, and 747-400. She holds a four year Business-Aviation degree from the University of Minnesota with the following pilot certificates and ratings: Airline Transport Pilot — Airplane Multi-engine Land, B757, B767, B747-400 type ratings; Commercial Privileges — Airplane Single Engine Land; Flight Engineer — Turbojet Powered; Gold Seal Flight Instructor — Airplane Single Engine Land, Multi-engine Land, & Instrument; Ground Instructor — Advanced & Instrument; Mechanic — Airframe & Powerplant; Restricted Radiotelephone operator; and First Class Medical Certificate.

Ms. Otypka is a member of the International Society of Women Airline Pilots (ISA), administering the printing and circulation of their newsletter and interviewing scholarship applicants. She is also a member of the Air Line Pilots Association (ALPA), the University Aviation Association (UAA), and Women in Aviation, Inc. (WAI). She is a former member of Aircraft Owners and Pilots Association (AOPA), the Experimental Aircraft Association (EAA), The Ninety-Nines, Inc. (99's), and has been an Aviation Explorer Scout counselor.

When not flying, Sylvia enjoys reading, writing, investment strategy, traveling, and pistol shooting (she is a member of the Women's Shooting Sports Foundation). Ms. Otypka resides in Aurora, Colorado. If you are interested in how she became a pilot, see *One Pilot's Career Path* in this book.

FOREWORD

Having played a principal role in the hiring of several thousand pilots for a major airline over the past 20 years I am often asked several questions regarding a piloting career with a major airline. The first two questions are: "how can I obtain an interview with your airline?" and "how can I ensure success in your employment process?" The third most frequently asked question is: "what exactly is your airline looking for?"

The answer to the first two questions is the same — *PREPARATION.* This book provides a lot of detailed information about how to prepare. There are many avenues one can take and many organizations willing to help. You can find the details in the book.

The third question is a little more difficult to answer. At our airline, we are attempting to hire *dedicated, professional pilots.* We attempt to measure your dedication and professionalism by looking at what you have done through preparation. Do you have a consistent educational and work history, always trying to *excel?* Have you always tried to stay in the industry, attempting to better your position and experience? Can you demonstrate that you have developed good leadership and decision making skills? Are you good at working with other people, particularly in a crew situation? We find that the best predictor of future success is one's past performance. We will explore this in depth in making the final employment decision.

Becoming an airline pilot is obviously a very challenging and formidable goal. For those who succeed, it is a very rewarding career. This book mentions a number of admirable role models, including the author. Ms. Otypka provides some excellent advice to the aspiring pilot in terms of what they need to do to prepare themselves for a career in aviation. She also provides impressive details about the many resources available to prospective pilots.

Captain William H. Traub
Vice President
Flight Standards and Training
United Airlines

INTRODUCTION

You're looking in the mirror while adjusting your tie and your crisp, white shirt. You brush off a speck of lint on your epaulets, then throw on your jacket with the four gold bars on the sleeves. Grabbing your suitcase and hat, you kiss your spouse good-bye and jump into the old beater, leaving the new car in the garage so it won't get jet-fuel-slimmed sitting in the parking lot at work. Once there, you check the weather and see that the usual line of thunderstorms will be waiting for you over the equator. You're an airline pilot and fly the biggest, most sophisticated airliner in the world. It's your dream job come true! How did you get here or how would you, if this wasn't the story of your life?

ED...THE LITTLE LADY WANTS TO KNOW
IF WE HAVE FLYING SAUCER RATINGS?

CHAPTER 1

So You Want to Fly
The Big Birds?

Have you ever dreamed about becoming an Airline Pilot? It takes a lot of dedication, but you can do it! You can make your dream come true. Even if it seems like a formidable task to get there, give it a try, you might surprise yourself. It's like becoming a doctor or lawyer, and it's a lot of fun. Think of your most favorite past time (hopefully flying) then think about getting to do it all the time — it's like being a kid in a candy store.

Let's begin with the basics:

Start early

Programs are available that you can become involved in that give you a taste of aviation at an early age. The EAA (Experimental Aircraft Association) has a Young Eagles program for ages 8 to 17. Young women and men that are ages 14 to 20 can become involved in Aviation Explorers, a program through the Boy Scouts. The Civil Air Patrol (CAP) has a Cadet program for ages 13 to 21.

Missions in Space, a space camp for fourth-graders and higher is available through 4-H Youth Programs, which are involved in aviation and space education. OBAP (Organization of Black Airline Pilots) sponsors young African American high school students to participate in a summer flight academy. Opportunity Skyway focuses on preparing minority and disadvantaged youngsters for a range of careers in aeronautics and transportation. Through their clubs they organize orientation flights, tours, career days, and private pilot ground school. (See Appendix: Organizations and Informational Sources, as well as other organizations that offer educational programs, speakers' banks, workshops, and career fairs.)

If it's too late to start early, that's OK. Age is no longer a factor. The airlines hire people into their mid-fifties. (Mandatory retirement age is 60.)

Stay away from drugs and alcohol

Anyone who feels that they can do both flying and drugs is in the wrong profession — it won't work and it *will* ruin your whole career. If you get a DUI, driving a car under the influence of alcohol, you may eventually be hired by the airlines, but those that don't have a mark on their record will be hired before you. If you have a pilot license now and get in trouble, your license can be suspended or revoked.

Maintain your health

Airlines look for healthy people who are not obese or anorexic. Protect and maintain your health. Wear safety glasses to protect your eyes if you work around any machinery — even just mowing the lawn. You can have many careers if you lose an eye but flying is not one of them. If your eyes aren't perfect, get some books on eye exercises or see a vision therapist and work on improving them. But *stay away* from any Laser retinal eye surgery, that is, Radial Keratotomy. This treatment is *absolutely disqualifying* for the military and for most airlines.

Get good grades

Working hard in school shows you can do the book work when training at the airlines. A college degree is no longer a requirement at most airlines, but it shows you can go the extra mile, are capable of higher learning, and are dedicated enough to complete your education. This will help you lead the pack in getting hired by an airline.

Routes to take

There are several ways to get into flying. If you want to fly the *really* Big Birds, jump in your DeLorean time machine, *slide* three to four hundred years *back to the future*, and attend Starfleet Academy. But if you want to stay in this space-time continuum, there are two more conventional routes to go and I will thoroughly discuss each: civilian and the military.

CHAPTER 2

THE CIVILIAN ROUTE

College

There are many universities available that combine obtaining your pilot licenses with studying for a degree. Be sure to look for schools that have an aviation curriculum that offers internship programs with the airlines. As an intern you earn credits working for one semester at an airline, either in the training center or flight office. This is an opportunity of a lifetime! It will give you exposure to the airlines, a look at the lifestyles of airline pilots, and simulator time in transport category aircraft. Most airlines will let you fly the simulator on your free time (these are $35 million dollar video games). At the completion of the semester, you usually receive a flight engineer rating or type rating along with a pilot interview with that airline at a later date.

As mentioned previously, a four year college degree is no longer a requirement for getting an airline job. However, 90% of the pilots hired by a major have a degree. This is a very important qualification to have when applying with an airline. Because aviation is such a dynamic profession it is also beneficial to develop management skills or have some other area of expertise as a backup if the airlines have layoffs, go bankrupt, or you lose your medical certificate.

Check out several colleges (and flight schools) before choosing one and talk to a career counselor. If there is a university you really want to attend which does not have an aviation program, look for alternative programs that may give you some credits for getting your pilot certificates. (See Appendix: Career Opportunities, Education & Flight Schools, and Scholarships).

Student Pilot Certificate

This is the starting point to becoming a pilot. You must be 16 years old (or 14 if you fly a glider or free balloon); need to read, speak, and understand the English language; and hold at least a third class medical certificate. The requirements for a third class medical are: vision of 20/40 with or without correction, color vision necessary for performance of duties (i.e., red and green color distinction), and good hearing. Also, you must be in good physical health and have no psychoses, alcohol, or drug dependency. The medical certificate is valid for three years if you are under the age of 40 or for two years if over 40.

Flying lessons may be started at a younger age, provided an instructor is always aboard the aircraft. Once you learn the basics, your instructor will sign you off to solo an aircraft. To solo, you must be 16 and you will be restricted from carrying passengers or property and flying in bad weather or at night (except in the airport area). This is a license to learn. (See Appendix: Training Products — FARs.)

Recreational Pilot Certificate

You must be 17 years old and meet the student pilot certification requirements as well as pass written, oral and flight tests. The minimum number of flight hours is 30: 15 hours of flight instruction and 15 hours of solo flight time. Like all

Jennifer Van Dyne instructing Laura Smith
before her first solo flight on her sixteenth birthday

certificates, this is the minimum time, so when checking flight schools and costs, ask what the average time is and the typical amount of money required, it's usually a lot more.

This is a very conditional license, since you can only fly within 50 miles of where you were instructed and only carry one passenger. Also, you are restricted to flying fixed gear airplanes with less than 180 horsepower that hold fewer than four people.

Private Pilot Certificate

You must be 17 years old (or 16 for a glider or free balloon rating) and in addition to the student pilot requirements you must pass written, oral, and flight tests. The minimums are 40 hours of flight training with 20 of them solo flight. For FAR (Federal Aviation Regulation) Part 141 schools, the requirements are 35 hours of ground school and 35 hours flight training, with 20 of those dual instruction, and 15 hours solo flight. Most flight schools are Part 141.

These are the *minimums* and with the complex environment we live in it may take many more hours of learning and experience before you feel ready for your flight test. If you have trouble hitting the books, do at least half of the ground instruction first, and reward yourself with the flight training. Many careers have stalled indefinitely because a pilot was ready for the flight test but never got around to study for and take the written test. The written test results are good for two years, whereas your flying competency will deteriorate quickly without practice. Put aside enough money and time for the entire course so you do not hinder your career. Remember, do not go by the minimums, look at the averages and know yourself. Are you are a slow, meticulous learner who takes time to learn new skills, or are you are a quick learner, where everything comes easily, or someone in-between? (See Appendix: Education & Flight Schools and Scholarships).

Instrument Rating

To secure this rating, you must have at least a Private Pilot Certificate and all the requirements that go with it and pass written and flight tests. The following flight experience is also needed: 125 hours of total flight time, with 50 hours pilot in command cross country (student pilot cross country does not count), and 40 hours of instrument time (maximum of 20 hours in a simulator). You also need 15 hours of instrument flight instruction with at least 5 of those hours in an airplane. Now you can fly in the clouds, but to be paid for it you need the next license.

Commercial Certificate

To obtain this certificate you must be at least 18 years old, pass written, oral and flight tests, and hold a second class medical certificate. The medical is the same as a third class except the distant vision requirement is 20/20 with or without correction, near vision is 20/40 with or without correction, and the medical is valid for only one year. The following flight experience is also a requisite: 250 hours of flight time (maximum of 50 hours in simulators), of which 100 hours must be in powered aircraft (can't be all in gliders), along with 50 hours in airplanes, and 10 hours in high performance airplanes. You also need 50 hours of flight instruction, of which 10 are instrument instruction (half must be in airplanes) and 10 are in preparation for the commercial flight test. Additional requirements are 100 hours of pilot in command time, with 50 cross-country, 50 in airplanes, and 5 at night. For a FAR Part 141 school you only need 190 hours total time (maximum of 40 hours in a simulator), with 100 hours solo, and 40 cross country.

Now you're ready to fly for a living..., well, not quite.

Building Flight Time

With what is considered very low flight time, it will be difficult to talk someone into hiring you. But don't despair — and be creative. There are ways to build flight time and experience both for the commercial certificate and subsequent ratings. Take an aerobatics course and learn how to fly unusual attitudes or get a glider rating. These experiences may come in handy someday in an emergency. Remember the Boeing 767 that ran out of fuel and landed on a drag strip in Canada? The Captain was a glider pilot.

Learning a variety of different piloting skills is a lot of fun. Get a float plane (seaplane), rotorcraft (helicopter), or hot air balloon rating. Learn to fly tail-draggers (tailwheel airplanes), or if you live in a cold part of the country, a ski plane. Compete in air races, or fly blood for the Red Cross or daffodils for the American Cancer Society. Tow gliders or banners, fly parachute jumpers or sightseeing trips, or perform aerial photography or survey. Fly pipeline or power line patrol, fish and wildlife-spotting, or participate in cloud-seeding projects. Become a ferry pilot, do pilot services, fire fighting, or crop dusting (agricultural pilot or aerial applicator).

Aero Care Lear Jet 35A
Charter and Aeromedical services

Fire fighting is a complex career in itself. And if you are interested in crop dusting, you need a commercial license, must take a skill and knowledge test of aerial application given by the FAA, and become licensed by the state. FAR 137 covers agricultural pilots. FAR 119.1 lists all the flying activities you can do under FAR Part 91. Information on pilot positions with Federal agencies may be found at the local federal employment office or by contacting each agency's regional office. (See Appendix: Career Opportunities).

But probably the fastest way to build up flight time is by becoming a flight instructor.

Flight Instructor Certificate

The minimum requirements for a flight instructor are: that you be 18 years old, hold a commercial certificate (including the second class medical), an instrument rating, and pass written, oral, and flight tests. Instrument instructor and multi-engine instructor are some additional ratings you should add to your certificate. The multi-engine instructor rating really comes in handy with pilots that have just bought an airplane, have their multi-rating, but not enough hours to satisfy the insurance requirements. So they need a flight instructor to fly with them for ten, twenty, or even fifty hours.

Something else that looks good on resumes and can help get your foot in the door for a flight instructor job is the ground instructor certificates: basic, advanced, and instrument. To get these you need only take a written test for each.

Although there are usually few, if any benefits with a company, flight instructing is not typically a lifetime vocation, but a stepping stone to help advance your flying career. Once you start instructing others, your flight time begins to accumulate quickly and teaching helps you learn more yourself.

Multi-engine Rating

The FAA has no minimum requirements for getting the multi-engine rating. This is an important rating to have in order to secure a commercial flying job. (Building multi-engine time is crucial to getting hired by a commuter airline and by the major airlines.) Typically it takes five to fifteen hours of flight training with an instructor to prepare for the checkride.

Commercial Flying & Commuter Flying

Now you can move on to flying commercially under FAR Part 135. For this you need a minimum of 500 hours to fly VFR/VMC (under visual flight rules or in visual meteorological conditions) and 1200 hours to fly IFR/IMC (under instrument flight rules or in instrument meteorological conditions). Usually it is difficult to get a 135 job unless you have 1200 hours and a multi-engine rating. However, some companies will hire you as a co-pilot with less time. You can also convince certain corporations that it would be to their advantage to have a co-pilot and that you happen to know where they can get one! Part 135 companies are air taxi operators (charter), freight and mail transportation, and commuters that hold less than 20 passengers.

Some commuters and Part 135 operators have a *pay to fly* program. This is where a person with low flight time will *pay* the company for the privilege to fly co-pilot for them. Some pilots from outside the US find this a good deal because flying is so expensive in their country. Others have enough money to partake and feel they can build up their flight time quicker. Law suits have stopped some of this practice in the past, however it still continues. This is a serious political and moral dilemma. If you do participate in this program you are taking away job opportunities for others and even for yourself in the future.

Typically a commuter airline will hire pilots who have about 2000 hours, with 500 to 700 hours multi-engine time. When the major airlines are doing extensive hiring, the commuter airlines have fewer pilots to choose from and will hire people with less flight time (about 1000 hours). The opposite is true when the majors haven't been hiring in several years. Working for a regional commuter airline, the starting pay can be as little as $10,000 a year for a first officer, but usually it's about $20,000.

Most commuters fly turbo-prop airplanes with some jets, but the trend is moving toward more regional jets (RJs - small jets holding up to 70 passengers). With this move to RJs, come higher salaries and more permanent careers. The salaries can be as high as $45,000 for a three-year first officer and $80,000 for a three-year Captain. With such favorable salaries it can be difficult to leave the commuter and start at a lower pay at the majors. But if you really want to fly the big birds you need to make this sacrifice. The higher pay potential is worth it, as well as the better benefits and generally increased stability and longevity.

The best way to find any of these jobs is by networking. For example: I was flying part time as a co-pilot for a corporation and heard about a full time job opening at a town I

First Officer David Stickler welcomes you
aboard a Mesa Airlines Beech 1900

visited. I got a job there flight instructing and flying canceled checks in a single engine airplane (VFR Part 135). When I went to the FAA to get my 135 *check out* (test), the examiner was impressed and he called me when he heard about a job flying twin engine airplanes. That got me a night freight flying job. Then a friend told me about a commuter that was hiring pilots.

Remember, all your flight time and experiences are cumulative. One job qualifies you for the next one and you slowly build up your flying credentials. (See Appendix: Career Opportunities.)

Airline Transport Pilot Certificate (ATP)

Get this immediately, when you have the minimum flight time, it's the most impressive rating to have and tells people that you are really serious. You must be at least 23 years old, be a high school graduate or equivalent, and most of all, be of good moral character (whatever that means — but this is taken very seriously). You also need a first class medical, which is valid for six months. The vision requirements are the same as for a commercial certificate, with intermediate vision stipulations of 20/40 with or without lenses. Normal color vision is a prerequisite, along with good hearing, an EKG Electrocardiogram at age 35 and yearly after age 40, and no psychosis, alcohol, or drug dependence. Basically you need to be in good physical health. Also you must pass the usual written, oral, and flight tests. You need a total time of at least 1500 hours: 500 hours cross-country and 250 hours pilot in command time (of which 100 hours are cross-country and 25 hours night time). Additional requirements are a total of 100 hours of night flight and 75 hours of instrument time.

Flight Currency Requirements

To maintain currency in an aircraft and carry passengers you must make three takeoffs and landings within a 90 period. To fly passengers at night, you also need three takeoffs and landings at night within 90 days. For IFR flying you must log six hours of instrument time with six instrument approaches every six months. If your instrument experience lapse, you are restricted to flying VFR only, until you complete an instrument competency check.

Once every 24 months you need a flight review. A Biannual flight review consists of at least one hour of flight instruction and one hour of ground instruction. You are exempt from this if you add another certificate or rating to your license during this period. The two year count down will start again after your checkride. (If you are flying Part 121 or Part 135 these requirements do not apply because you will have six month and yearly checks by your employer.)

The flight instructor certificate is the only pilot license that must be renewed every two years or it expires and you must take a checkride again. There are three ways to renew your certificate. Within 90 days of expiration you can take a flight instructor refresher course (these are offered on weekends all over the country). You can go to the FAA, show your records of instructing students, and prove that you are a competent instructor by the number of your students that passed their checkrides. Or you can show records that you are a company check pilot, chief flight instructor, or fly Captain under FAR Part 121.

CHAPTER 3

THE MILITARY ROUTE

To fly for the military you must be an officer and to become an officer you must have a four year degree. But how do you know if you want to make this commitment? There are four routes to take, lets look at each of them. The paths with the Air Force, Navy, and Marines are similar. We'll use the Air Force circuit as an example.

United States Air Force Academy (USAF)

The first possible route is to get a service appointment at the USAF Academy at Colorado Springs. Approximately 1200 students enter the Academy each year. The minority enrollment is 17 percent, including 12 percent women (this year they had 19 percent women, the highest number in history). The Academy environment has a highly structured military atmosphere.

You need to start thinking about the Academy in your sophomore year in high school. The recommended high school courses to take are: four years of English; four years of math, including algebra, geometry, trigonometry, calculus and functional analysis; sciences — biology, chemistry, physics, and computers; social sciences — history, economics, government and behavioral science; and two or three years of a foreign language — either German, French, Spanish, Russian, Chinese, Japanese, or Arabic.

Scheduling a PLAN/PACT (Preliminary American College Test) or PSAT (Preliminary Scholastic Aptitude Test) as a sophomore is highly recommended. These scores are needed for the pre-candidate questionnaire (PCQ). (Get a PCQ and request a service application early in your junior year of high school.) To be competitive you should obtain scores of 58 verbal and 56 math for the PSAT or 24 composite for the PACT/PLAN. This way you can improve any low scores before taking the Scholastic Aptitude Test (SAT) and/or the American College Test (ACT).

The SAT and ACT can be retaken as often as you wish, as the highest scores from either test will be used. SAT scores usually improve 50 points when testing the second time. The SAT or ACT should be taken in your junior year. One of these tests is required for all candidates. The average SAT scores of candidates is: verbal — 520 to 600 and math — 610 to 700. The average ACT scores are: English — 25 to 29, reading — 26 to 33, math — 26 to 30, and science reasoning — 26 to 31.

Grade point average (GPA) should be 3.8-4.0 (out of 4.0), with some exceptions of 3.5-4.0. Athletics, social or leadership, and community involvement is just as important as academics. You must be between the ages of 17 and 22 years old, a US citizen, and of excellent moral character. Also, you must meet all the academic and physical requirements and must be single, with no children or dependents. The Air Force is looking for bright, healthy, well-rounded people.

If you can't quite get the grade point average and are an exceptional athlete, you can get in on what is similar to an athletic scholarship. The Air Force is very competitive and wants to have good people on their sports teams. First you must go to prep school, which is a conditional acceptance and if you perform successfully there, you can move on to the academy. Prep school is one year and stresses English, math,

The Air Force Academy, Colorado Springs, Colorado

chemistry, and military training. The Academy offers scholarships to seven civilian prep schools around the country. They are also made available for minorities and military enlisted personnel.

Each applicant must pass a Candidate Fitness Test (CFT). CFT averages for men are: 10 pull-ups, 69 sit-ups in 2 minutes, 41 push-ups in 2 minutes, and a 300 yard shuttle run in 60 seconds. For women these averages are: 2 pull-ups, 68 sit-ups, 24 push-ups, and 300 yards in 69 seconds. You can prepare for the CFT by building up strength and endurance through team sports like basketball and football, swimming and wrestling, and distance running and conditioning exercises. In addition, women need to increase upper-body strength to prepare for the test (at least one pull-up is required to pass). The PCQ offers preparation guidelines for the CFT (it also contains medical examination evaluations and waivers as well as a scheduling time table to complete all the requirements).

You can develop your leadership abilities through extracurricular activities, school clubs, class activities, academic societies, community groups, and work experiences.

To get an appointment you need a nomination from either your US Senator or US Representative of your state of residence. The Academy will give you instructions to help you with the nomination process. The prescribed time to apply for a nomination is the spring of your junior year in high school. The PCQ supplies guide-lines and sample letters to help you with this. Write a letter to your official, then set up a meeting, selling yourself with all of your qualifications and enthusiasm.

There are also 100 appointments made annually by the President and members of Congress for children of enlisted, warrant, and commissioned members of regular and reserve components. Children of deceased or disabled veterans have no limit to nominations and children of medal of honor recipients do not need appointments. One hundred seventy appointments are available annually for air force regulars and reservists. There are twenty appointments reserved for honor students in military schools. The Vice President may nominate candidates from the nation at large.

Admissions counseling assistance is available through the admission liaison officers (ALOs). Also, the academies encourage interested students to call and visit for a closer look. The other academies are: the US Military Academy at West Point and the US Naval (Marine) Academy at Annapolis. The US Coast Guard Academy at New London and the US Merchant Marine Academy at Kings Point have admission based on competitive examination, rather than nominations. (See Appendix: Military Contacts).

The academy takes care of all your education (free tuition, room, board, medical and dental care) and the only major expense for the student is a computer. Each cadet has his/her own computer and sends in their lessons on it. (A deposit of approximately $2500 is required to help pay for uniforms and other personal expenses, which is credited to your cadet account.) Everyone receives a monthly allowance, which is cadet pay.

The required curriculum includes professional courses in leadership, astronautics, law for commanders, military history, defense policy and light-plane flying. The academic load is heavy: 22 credit hours a semester, plus the military training. Instructors will give each student extra and individual study as necessary.

Summer aviation training is available that includes soaring, parachuting, navigation and pilot indoctrination. Instruction in a Slingsby T-3A Firefly is a prerequisite for selection to undergraduate pilot training. The T-3A is a British trainer that looks somewhat like a beefed-up Piper Tomahawk without a T-tail (260 horse-power, low-wing, fixed-gear, two-seater, with a bubble canopy and fully aerobatic). Primary training consists of 18 sorties or about 24 hours, with solo occurring in 17 hours.

The wash out rate in the academy is 50%, which usually happens within the first year or two. Because of the rigorous physical training and the structured system, the majority of cadets who wash out do so in the first month. After the completion of the second year, you must decide if this is the career you want to stay in and sign a commitment to the service. This commitment is ten years and starts after completing four years at the academy and one year of pilot training.

Officers Candidate School or Officers Training School (OCS/OTS)

The second potential route to take with the service is OCS or OTS. This is for people who already have a four year degree and it is best to apply in the fall of your senior year in college — see a local recruiter. When you sign up, *be sure* to sign a contract for *pilot training* and nothing else. A recruiter may tell you it's easy to transition, but in reality it is very difficult to move from one career field to another.

The only exception to getting into pilot training without a four year degree is the Army, which still takes two year degree officers for rotorcraft flying. But if you want to get into the airlines in the future, or most other flying careers, fixed wing aircraft is the way to go.

The requirements to become a commissioned officer are: 19 to 29 years old, height 4' 10" to 6' 8", weight commensurate to age and height, vision 20/20, and good health to pass the medical exam. You must also successfully complete the officer qualification test and be of good moral character (no court convictions, juvenile delinquency, arrest, or drug use). People who are single with one or more minor dependents are not eligible. Waivers are granted on a case-by-case basis to some requirements.

After being selected for OCS/OTS, you join the enlisted ranks for the duration of your training, which lasts 12 to 20 weeks. Basic officer training covers the roles and responsibilities of an officer, military laws and regulations, military polices, leadership, and physical training. Then it's on to pilot instruction.

Pilot training

Pilot training is a structured qualification and elimination process. You begin with the enhanced flight screening program (sometimes refer to as *FISH POT*). Here you will fly eighteen sorties in a Slingsby T-3A Firefly. This is about twenty hours of flight instruction with a solo at fifteen hours. You must complete the syllabus of training to acceptable standards or you are washed-out of the program. This is the same training as in the USAF Academy. (The flight time is slightly lower because it takes less time to fly out to the practice area.) All primary training and evaluation for OTS, ROTC (Reserve Officers Training Corps), the Reserves or the Guard is done in Hondo, Texas (near San Antonio) by civilians.

The flight training then continues with flying up to three times a day. If you have a bad day and bust two qualifications

Marilyn Koon flying T-38 supersonic jet trainers

you go up to the elimination board, where they will work out your fate. If you washout, it does not mean you can't fly airplanes or are a bad pilot, but only that you can't keep up with the rigorous pressure set forth in service training.

After basic flight training, you learn to fly a subsonic jet, then either go to supersonic jets (fighters) or multi-engine transports. If you are looking down the road to a career with the airlines, the best option is to fly the transport aircraft. To transition from single seat fighters to a crew concept airline is more difficult and having already done this in the service looks good on your resume. However, if your life will never be complete because you forced yourself to pass up a fighter pilot position, than by all means, be true to yourself. Lots of airline pilots have come from the fighter pilot ranks. Be aware that you will not gain as much flight time flying this kind of aircraft and flight time is one of the considerations when applying to the airlines.

The transports usually carry a crew of four or eight to ten. You learn crew coordination and a lifestyle that is more comparable to the airlines. You may be on the road 220 days out of the year and fly air refueling, cargo and passengers to almost every country in the world. After 1000 hours of flight time (about two years) and depending on availability and aircraft, you upgrade to captain. Again, this is a ten year commitment beginning after pilot training. The wash out rate is 33% to 50%, but keep yourself focused on the success rate: 50% to 65%.

Officers' pay is based on basic pay, incentives and special pay. As a pilot you will get basic pay and incentives. First year basic pay is $19,000 to $22,000. Pay grades increase by promotions and rank. You can live free of charge in military housing on your assigned base or receive a housing allowance. Other benefits include health care, Veterans' benefits and an excellent retirement program.

For pilot training in the Navy-Marine Corps, preflight indoctrination is done in Pensacola, Florida. Basic flight training continues in Pensacola or in Corpus Christi, Texas. Advanced training is accomplished in Pensacola; Corpus Christi; Meridian, Mississippi; or Beeville, Texas. Pilot training takes 18 to 24 months.

Reserve Officers Training Corps (ROTC)

The third way to get into the military is by becoming involved in the ROTC. These programs are available at many colleges and universities. You must be a US citizen, between the ages of 17 and 21 years old, a high school graduate or possess an equivalency certificate, physically qualified, be able to bear arms, pass the Officer Qualifying Test (OQT), be interviewed and selected by a board, and complete a four week field training course.

There are one, two and four year programs with financial scholarships available for tuition, books, fees, uniforms, and a monthly allowance ($150 per month). Scholarships are usually for two or three years. The minimum GPA for non-technical majors is 3.0 while the minimum GPA for minority students or technical majors (such as physics or math) is 2.65. A scholarship board meets after each semester for scholarships to begin the next fall. The scholarships for minorities or technical majors are not required to meet a board and selections are made throughout the year. Air Force ROTC offers a non-competitive scholarship of $2000 per year plus $150 per month for all juniors and seniors with a 2.35 GPA.

Four year scholarships are available to high school seniors. For this you need to talk to a local recruiter during the spring of your junior year and pick up an application. Your high school GPA must be 2.5 or higher, class standing in top 25% (can get a waiver for this), with a qualifying SAT — math at least 500, verbal at least 450 and a total of 1000. For ACT you need a math score of at least 21, verbal at least 21, and composite of 24. You cannot be a single parent.

Most students can try ROTC for a year without making any commitment to join (you must join by your junior year). When you join, be sure the military needs pilots and that you have a good chance of getting into pilot training. Also, sign up at the ROTC detachment on campus, not with a recruiter. To get into flight training you need a GPA of at least 3.0 and social or leadership skills. So you need to be involved in a club, fraternity, or sorority. A private pilot license is recommended but not required.

A pilot candidate completes Air Force sponsored training prior to their senior year of college. This includes basic aerodynamics, aircraft systems, emergency procedures, flight training and solo flights.

As with every career, there are shortages and surpluses and timing is everything. ROTC courses are like other college electives and contain the basic officers training course (leadership training classes included), along with drills for several hours each week and military training exercises for several weeks each summer. ROTC graduates are commissioned as a second lieutenant with an annual salary of $24,000, four weeks paid annual leave, and medical benefits. You serve full-time for seven years, after one year of pilot training, or a total of eight years. (See Appendix: Military Contacts — ROTC).

Air National Guard or Reserves

This fourth military connection is one that may appeal to many people. Find a base where you like living, which has airplanes you want to fly and become committed to it (changing bases is very difficult). In the interview process you need to determine if you like this group while they decide if they approve of you. The base prefers to groom and *home grow* their people.

Timing is also important. The best way to start is right out of high school. While you are working part time with the reserves, work full time on your degree. The guard and reserves have financial scholarships available. To give you experience with aircraft, apply for jobs in maintenance, as crew chief, or on the flight line. Also work on getting some flying experience. This shows you are motivated and really want to fly for a living. Accumulate one to two hundred hours of flight time. This will give you an edge to getting into pilot training (the failure rate from pilot training is lower for those candidates having some flying experience). Many bases have flying clubs, so you can learn to fly there, otherwise you need to go to a civilian airport and local FBO (fixed base operator or flight school).

When you complete your four year degree, request to go to pilot training. The pilot training is the same as previously mentioned. You need to complete an application, an aviation aptitude test, and an interview with your squadron. They look at your leadership skills, learning abilities, and tactical abilities. If you are known on the base as a sharp, hard working individual this will go a long way at the review board. The flight squadron will then make a recommendation to the headquarters board, who makes the final determination. The board meets two to four times a year. Currently they sanction

Two Colorado Air National Guard F-16s

40 to 50 pilots for training each year. This is their quota, which may vary from year to year. Fifty percent of those recommended come from within the reserve units and fifty percent come via interviewing pilots from off the street (usually pilots that have previous military experience). The Air National Guard has a similar program.

After flight training you have a seven year, part time commitment as a *weekend warrior*. Some people use the military as a full time job, making themselves available to fly whenever trips are open. (They are called reserve or guard *bums*.) This is a way to build up your flight time quicker. Another option is to be hired full time in a civil service position as an ART or AGT (air reserve technician or air guard technician). This job is a combination of a staff and flying job. The civil service route is generally for those who want a life-time career and if you leave after a few years you need to be very diplomatic or you may ruffle some feathers.

As in many aviation sectors, the military is an ever-changing environment, and has revised its requirements and duty commitments many times due to changing needs. So be sure to check what the current commitments are.

For many, the military life agrees with them and they serve out a full career, retire, then start a second career in the airlines. But what some people forget when participating in the regular service and especially the reserves, is that if there is a war (like the Gulf War) you can and may be called into active service and fighting. (See Appendix: Military Contacts.)

CHAPTER 4

GETTING THE AIRLINE JOB

You are ready to start looking for an airline job. You have kept an accurate, neat logbook of all your flying experience. You have a degree, all the pilot ratings, certificates, and flight time you can get and feel ready to tackle the Big Boys. So where do you start? The best place is the Appendix. Check out every resource available to help you find out which airlines are hiring and what requirements are necessary. You should do this investigating while you are building your flight time so you know what to be aiming for.

Books

Read books on resume and cover letter writing, networking, interviewing, and dress for success. This industry is unique, but there is a lot of basic data in many books that will be helpful for any profession. You can never be too knowledgeable or do too much research. Several companies have information available that is specifically tailored to getting an airline job. (Review the Foreword. See Appendix: Career Opportunities, Interviewing Resources, Organizations & Informational Sources, and Training Products.)

Networking

Do lots of it. Talk to every pilot you know and find out what they know about the airlines. When you fly as a passenger, stop in the cockpit before or after the flight and talk to the pilots. (Before is preferable, because a lot of times pilots have other planes to catch too.) Although it may be more impressive to talk with the Captain, she/he is the most senior pilot and has been out of the hiring mode the longest. It's usually more advantageous to talk with the most junior pilot. Ask him/her when they were hired, what their qualifications were, if their airline is hiring now, and what kind of people they employ.

Get a *strong* letter of recommendation from a pilot you know, preferably someone you have flown with a lot. Find someone you have known professionally for a considerable amount of time and have them provide specifics about you that may not show on your application or may not come up in the interview. Many airlines have recommendation forms for the pilots working there which they can fill out and you can submit with your application. It is acceptable to have additional attachments added to the form and this extra information is welcome and will be considered with your application. At some airlines, a recommendation form can get you an interview with that airline and a *strong* recommendation can mean the difference between getting the job or being passed by because someone else gave a better interview or an exceptional flight test.

The airlines are looking not only for people with good flying skills, but pilots that can incorporate those skills with crew-coordination. Even if you have not participated much in a crew environment, it is important to have leadership and decision making abilities, proficient communication skills, a positive attitude, and good learning capabilities.

Each airline wants everyone to fit into its own particular mold. Some favor military pilots and others prefer civilians. A few airlines are really laid back, while certain companies are very stuffy or very, very conservative, and others are less conservative. That's why it's best to apply to as many airlines as possible, to find one that fits. That is also why you may interview with several companies before being offered a job, so don't despair, and keep on trying.

WELL, IT LOOKS LIKE YOU'RE JUST THE PILOT WE'RE
LOOKING FOR...WE THINK YOU'LL FIT IN REAL WELL

CHAPTER 5

THE INTERVIEW

The hiring process

The hiring process for most airlines is a combination of aptitude, medical and flight tests, and the interview. There may be more than one interview and many airlines conduct the second interview with a pilot (usually a Captain) and someone from Human Resources or employment personnel. Having to perform in front of two people is more stressful, but is usually the norm. The interviewers may appear a little stiff. They are trained to avoid developing excessive rapport, which could result in conveying to the candidate that part of the evaluation is based on personality or give them a false sense of hope. They also do not want to be so empathetic and friendly that it becomes difficult to make an objective decision. Interviewers are schooled to avoid behavior that might influence the candidate's responses, such as nodding their head and agreeing with the applicant's answer. They try to keep non-interview-related dialogue to a minimum. So expect severe-looking interviewers.

Before the interview

Before the interview, the interviewer reviews the candidates' credentials. They examine the application for typing, completion, and following directions. Dates of employment should match on each document. All questions must be answered and qualifications or experience should not be misrepresented. Employment and work history should demonstrate career progression, stability, and responsible positions. Frequent employment changes or changes that resulted in lateral or backward movement in terms of job complexity and responsibility will be questioned. Be honest in your explanations and do not be defensive about such changes. Also, all termination's will be questioned so be prepared to clarify these.

It is important to depict a continual progression in aviation. This shows persistence and motivation. (If you need to do some other kind of work to support yourself, try to remain in the aviation field.) The interviewer will search for dependability and behavioral characteristics by looking for excessive illnesses, absences, and tardiness. They will also investigate moving violations on driving records (no offense in the last three years shows that you are a responsible person) and check for DUIs/DWIs, felonies and misdemeanors. Education should have minimum, if any institutional changes and should exhibit consistent academic performance (transcripts, grade point average and academic focus). Also, the purpose for your college major may be examined and reasons why you did not attend college or why you began but did not complete it.

The interview structure

The interview is conducted in a structured way, which usually starts with establishing rapport. The interviewers set a friendly and informal tone with a smile, a hand shake, and a conversational style. They will then set the stage for the interview by explaining the purpose of the interview, the nature of their role, and the place of the interview in the overall selection process. They usually explain the amount of time the interview will take and that they will be taking notes. The interviewers will ask open-ended questions that encourage the candidate to open up and be talkative. They will tolerate silence by being quiet and giving the applicant a chance to think (usually 15 seconds, which is a long time). They will seek information regarding your assets and liabilities, challenges and problems, and successes and failures. They will also ask follow-up questions, particularly if your responses are vague. The interviewers will observe how you communicate non-verbally through posture, eye contact, body movements, facial expressions and gestures. They will then close the interview by asking you if you have any questions for them and tell you when you will be contacted.

A typical interview

An example of a typical interview may be broken down into six categories. The first one is presentation: personal appearance and manner, good self expression, good first impression, professional attitude, a courteous and considerate manner, and completion of submitted documents. Next will be an assessment of the applicant's general awareness of the industry and the airline itself. The third area could be about career planning and goals. Your responses to questions should reveal a commitment to a professional pilot career, sacrifices that have or will be made to achieve this goal, and career planning and goal-setting. Another category covered will be on technical knowledge. A demonstration of the knowledge of the current aircraft you fly (i.e., the maximum gross weight, approach speeds, stall speeds, etc.), familiarity of the FARs, operational judgment, and an explanation of any accidents, incidents, or violations (it's best to have none of these). Your logbooks will be reviewed and open ended questions such as explaining the fire procedure of your aircraft, radio failure procedures, and a discussion of windshear alert actions may be covered. The next category will go over your personal strengths and weaknesses to see if you exhibit self knowledge and display a take-charge attitude. The last area covered may be about your interpersonal skills: the importance of communication, team building capabilities, confidence or arrogance, sensitivity and modesty, and good eye contact. (See Appendix: Interviewing Resources).

Illegal topics

Questions and topics that should not be explored are issues of legality (age, race, religion, marital status, spouse's employment, child care arrangements, number of children, plans to have children, parent's employment, friends or relatives working for company, living arrangements, sexual orientation, credit history, etc.) or issues of job-relatedness (appearance, personal traits or characteristics, personal preferences, or general attitudes). Appearance should be an important consideration only as it relates to professionalism.

DON'T LAUGH... HE'S THE SENIOR PILOT AND
MAKES MORE THAN THE TWO OF US PUT TOGETHER

CHAPTER **6**

FLYING THE BIG BIRDS
THE LIFE OF AN AIRLINE PILOT

What should you expect when you finally get an airline job?

The Myths

The flying public think airline pilots (even commuter pilots) receive a salary of $250,000 a year and fly free anywhere in the world first class. They never work and when they do, they only go to exotic places and stay there for days sitting on the beach or by the pool.

The Reality
Salaries

In reality it takes a lot of hard work and sometimes very little pay for years before being hired by a major airline. Starting salaries at major airlines are in the neighborhood of $26-33,000. Only the top ten percent make $175,000 to $200,000 and very rarely $250,000. To be in that category requires a lot of seniority, which translates into many years with the airline, and that means you are getting close to retirement and the end of your career.

Benefits

Most major airlines offer exceptional health, retirement, and flight benefits. You can usually expect full medical and dental plans, life insurance, sick leave benefits, and a company sponsored retirement fund with an optional employee sponsored retirement fund (i.e., 401K). Pass privileges (flight benefits) are available to your spouse, parents, and children.

The *free flying* really means flying standby with lots of backups and sometimes getting the last middle seat on the airplane. If you go to Hawaii, Europe, Australia, or other favorite destinations, you may never get there, especially during popular times of the year. Of course it is wonderful to pop off to LA for dinner!

Commuting

Unlike most careers, with a flying job you do not have to live and work in the same city, state, or even country. Each airline has *pilot bases* or *domiciles*, cities where pilots start their flying from. It makes your life much simpler to live in the same town you are based, but it is no longer a requirement. You can live virtually anywhere...as long as you always show up for work on time. Instead of taking a city bus to work like some people, you can take an Airbus or a Boeing!

It's nice to live where you want to, but with that comes the responsibility of being where you're supposed to be to fly your trips. Don't ruin the career of your dreams because of cavalier planning on your part. You need to provide lots of backups for yourself if your planned flight is full or gets cancelled due to weather or a mechanical problem.

Captain Jack Pendleton and First Officer Harry Gaines
flying a United Airlines Airbus 320

Work Schedule

The layovers in exotic places are wonderful: Paris, Singapore, the Bahamas. That's when you fly international. On domestic flying you may be in marvelous places like Fargo, Little Rock, or Buffalo (or Seattle, San Francisco, or Steamboat). All layovers are as minimal as possible for the company, so you may need to sleep through half or all the time you are there.

Flying internationally, you will have many days off every month, sometimes up to 20 (usually 16 to 18), but you get all your work done at once because you may be on duty 14 to 20 hours each day. Sometimes you need a couple of days off work just to get over the jet lag. Flying domestically, you usually have 12 to 16 days off, with work shifts that can be 10 to 14 hours long. And with all multi-day flying, you are away from home 200 to 300 hours a month. When you're on reserve, you are on call 24 hours a day, with 9 to 12 days free. Some of those days can be converted into working days if you fly internationally.

A typical day at work is not typical at all. If you fly domestically on a *narrow-body* aircraft (a smaller plane, i.e., a Boeing 737 or MD-80) you may fly four to eight *legs* a day. (A leg is a segment of a trip: Chicago to Denver is one leg and Denver to Tulsa is another leg.) On a three day trip you may have one long *layover* (overnight stay) of 15 to 20 hours, followed by another day of flying and a short layover of 10 to 12 hours. On the last day of a trip you will usually start very early and be finished flying in the early afternoon.

Domestic flying on a *wide-body* or large aircraft (Boeing 767, 777, or DC-10) has longer trips with frequent coast to coast flying where you only fly one or two legs a day. International flying on smaller aircraft is similar to domestic flying and many times domestic and international flying is mixed together in a trip (i.e., fly San Francisco to Los Angeles to Mexico City, layover, then fly back to the states). When you fly internationally on widebody aircraft like the Boeing 747 you usually only fly one leg a day, but that leg may be 15 hours long if you fly to Hong Kong.

Probation & Reserve

During your first year with an airline you will be on probation. Probation usually starts *after* you have completed all your training with the company. Since you are a *junior* pilot you will probably be on reserve too. Reserve means being on call and available 24 hours a day. You need a beeper, cellular phone, and/or telephone and you are responsible for every call the *crew desk* or crew scheduling makes to you. If your beeper doesn't go off and you miss a trip, you are responsible for the missed trip. On probation even one missed trip could cause you to lose your job. Most airlines take this very seriously. It only takes a few missed trips after probation to ruin a good career.

On probation you will usually get quarterly *line checks*. This is where a check airman rides with you on one of your legs and observes how you do your job. If you know your tasks and do them well, this is no big deal. If you are weak you will be counseled and possibly have to go in for recurrent training. Line checks are a way of life and all pilots have them once or twice a year.

If you are a commuter and on reserve, you need to be at your domicile on your reserve days. This means staying with family, friends, renting an apartment, or paying for a hotel room yourself. You could fly every reserve day and not have the cost of a place to stay or you could sit for days and weeks and not be called for a trip.

Some people hate reserve, while others enjoy the challenge and the diversity (you will work with a variety of crews and may fly out of several domiciles with different trips). Unless you are a senior pilot on reserve, you will usually fly a lot of weekends and holidays. Again, this is a bonus for some people: going skiing, traveling, and even to movies during your weekdays off frequently is more fun than competing with hordes of tourists.

Seniority & Bidding

Seniority is the airline pilot's life. Your monthly schedules and the aircraft you fly are all based on seniority. Each month a pilot *bids* for a schedule for the following month. *Lines* (monthly schedules) are printed and can be picked up in *flight-ops* (the flight operations area) or you can download them on to your computer. You select the trips or days off you want, find the lines that coincide with these and you put in a bid, specifying your first choice, second choice, etc. The schedules are awarded a few days later and it's like Christmas, you've written your list and checked it twice but won't know for sure what you got until the day the bid results are out.

The most wonderful part about bidding and seniority is that you can tailor your schedule to have time off while most people do not have that option. You can bid one month where you have the last week off and bid the following month with the first week off to give you two weeks or more free, creating a sabbatical. You can also stretch ten days of vacation into two or three weeks by bidding days off before and after your holiday.

After the first year with an airline (or more or less, depending on the rapidity of expansion of the company) you have many choices and you can cater your job to the lifestyle you want to live. You can spend your career always flying the biggest and highest paying airplane your seniority will allow and make the most money possible. The trade off is living on reserve, working holidays, and putting your social life second. This works well for some people.

For others the opposite is more appealing: being the most senior on an aircraft and having the first choice of days off and places to fly. This also means being home for most of the events in your family's lives, having holidays off, and layovers at those *exotic* places. The trade off is that you will be on a lower paid plane or seat (position), i.e., first officer or flight engineer to hold that seniority. And then somewhere in the middle works for others, at least you can choose and then choose again when your life changes. What ever lifestyle works for you, you'll be doing what you love to do and getting paid for it.

Initial Training

Another aspect of the airline pilot's job is training. When you are hired by an airline, they will train you to fly a specific airplane the way they want it flown (airlines all outfit their planes differently). Each company has standard operating procedures (SOPs) that it expects you to adhere to. Usually you only fly one type of airplane, i.e., the Boeing 727 until you bid onto another one, then you need to go back to school for that airplane. The training consists of about two weeks of ground school and two weeks of simulator flying. The check-ride includes a two hour oral and a four hour flight test. The flight test is done in the simulator and the first time you see the airplane is on your initial flight with passengers. (Talk

Japan Airlines Boeing 747-400 landing in Hong Kong

about virtual reality. These simulators are so sophisticated that if you have a major mishap while flying one, you'll feel as if you've really crashed.) On your first *line* trip (or work trip), which is usually about four days, you will have with you a check pilot who will keep a close watch on you. In essence, this is your final check-out or test.

There is also a new type of initial simulator training called AQP (Advance Qualification Program). This is very similar to the other training: you must successfully complete each phase and follow the training guidelines along with the maneuvers and procedures for each session. But when each maneuver is successfully completed, it will be signed off and you do not have to be tested on it again.

Recurrent Training

Once a year, or at certain airlines, twice a year, you go through recurrent training, called a Proficiency Check (PC). (Some airlines will call this annual training by a different name.) This is typically three days of training and flight checks in the simulator. The first day may encompass emergency evacuation and a two hour LOFT (Line Oriented Flight Training). A LOFT is a typical flight in the simulator from one city to the next but could become one of those *trips from hell* where everything goes wrong. The purpose of the LOFT is to test your CLR/CLM (Command Leadership Resource Management or Command Leadership Management) abilities. This is about working together in a crew concept or as a team. This is extremely important. Gone are the days of simple airplanes where the Captain was god and the rest of the crew was there for his bidding. In today's complex environment the crew must work together for the successful outcome of every flight, whether any problems arise or it's just a typical day.

The next day you will accomplish ditching training and practice flight maneuvers. Advanced maneuvers training (flying unusual attitudes) will also be covered. The third day consists of a two hour oral test, checking your knowledge of aircraft systems and operations. After the oral you will have a four hour flight check in the simulator. Then a review of windshear procedures will be covered.

With the initial AQP training comes its counterpart during recurrent training called CQP (Continued Qualification Program). This is similar to the regular PC but with a few changes. There is more emphasis on CLR/CLM during the LOFT. A program called first look is also incorporated. This is where you are graded as successful, marginally successful or unsuccessful on your first try of a maneuver. On day two, instead of practicing with an instructor you will work with a check airman and accomplish what is called MTV (not video rock and roll, but maneuvers training validation). If you successfully complete a maneuver (engine failure procedure on takeoff, a single engine approach, non-precision approach, go-around, etc.) she/he will *sign you off* and you will not have to be tested again the following day. The day three simulator check is a LOE (line orientated evaluation) which is flown more like a line trip than a test.

Along with the annual training some home study is required. There is usually a designated list of videos and slides to view, written tests to take, and your own personal review of the aircraft systems for the oral test. Semi-annually you must complete a written open book test. This is all to help you keep the sophisticated systems and emergency procedures fresh in your mind...just in case.

You must take a FAA physical annually or semi-annually to maintain your first or second class medical certificate. Most airlines also require its pilots to take a company physical annually, bi-annually, or in some cases every third year.

CHAPTER **7**

WOMEN IN THE AIRLINES

In 1929 there were 117 licensed women pilots in America. Today there are 40,000, 6% of the total 700,000 pilots. Only 2.5% of the ATP pilots or Airline Transport Rated pilots are women.

The first woman to be hired by an airline was Helen Richey in December 1934, by Central Airlines (which became North Central, then Republic, before merging with Northwest Orient). The company used her more as a public relations vehicle than as a pilot. The male pilots vehemently opposed her and blatantly discriminated against her, not letting her fly in bad weather and refusing to allow her to become a union member. Having only flown a dozen round trips, she resigned in less than a year, not wanting to be a fair weather pilot and publicity act.

The Airlines hired a few women aviators during World War II and thereafter, but employed them only as link trainer operators and when simulators replaced the link trainers, as simulator instructors. But in the United States, women had to wait 39 years before being hired again as airline pilots.

Captain Emily Howell Warner flying a Frontier Boeing 737

(Non-US carriers hired one woman in 1953, two in the late 1960's, and two in 1971 & 1972.)

On January 29, 1973, Frontier Airlines hired Emily Howell Warner. She had 7000 hours of flight time and had started applying with the airlines in 1967. It took over six years of sending out applications and resumes before one airline would notice her. Even then, she had to talk to the Vice President of Flight Operations before obtaining a formal interview. (Her uniform is in the Smithsonian Air and Space Museum in Washington DC.) American, TWA, Eastern, and Delta each hired one female pilot that year.

A handful of women pilots were hired in 1974, 1975, and 1976; and in 1977 almost two dozen were hired. In 1978 and 1979, females finally had more of an opportunity to get into the majors with almost 100 women being hired. Today there are 2000 women pilots (2500 world wide) flying for the major airlines, which makes up only 4% of the over 50,000 airline pilots in the United States, with less than 500 female Captains.

Why has it been so difficult for women to break into the aviation field? For some of the same reasons it has been hard for women to get into other male-dominated fields. The airlines argued that women would quit to start a family and therefore hiring women would not be cost effective. Also, minimum height requirements were set as high as five feet, eight inches. But the big problem was that attitudes needed to change. Equal rights activists lobbied the companies and law suits were successfully won. Today things are better and there are now several organizations that offer women support and encouragement. (See Appendix: Women's Organizations).

CHAPTER 8

WORKING WITH
"THE GOOD OLD BOYS"

A part of flying that is not unique to the airline industry is "The Good Old Boys Club." Some people deny that this club exists, and there are places where it is not so prevalent. However, women frequently find themselves feeling like outsiders in a male dominated career. Men can also feel this if they are *too old* or *too young*, from another country, or not Caucasian.

In a recent ISA (International Society of Women Airline Pilots) survey on gender discrimination and sexual oriented harassment, gender discrimination was found to be the more frequent and more significant of the two. This varied from verbal discrimination and stereo typing — "women don't belong in the cockpit" or "another empty kitchen" — to professional discrimination and shunning — refusal to accept your input and/or refusal to talk to you.

But sexual harassment is not dead. Sexual jokes, innuendo, comments, and unwanted advances and touching still happen. Fortunately it all happens less frequently as time goes by and more women become pilots. The airlines have taken some steps in addressing this issue through Crew Resource Management (CRM) and diversity training.

Harassment and discrimination have come out into the open and many pilots worry about it and think first before talking or touching.

No matter what your sex or color you may occasionally run across a pilot who is not easy to work with or get along with. This person may be very unhappy or you may push their buttons because you have the world at your feet and they don't. Sometimes a pilot needs to feel powerful and feed his/her ego by bossing junior pilots around. They can be rude, grumpy, or just uncooperative. Don't take it personally. Chances are he/she act that way with most pilots. The good news is that you only have to work with them for a few days or weeks instead of indefinitely at a conventional job.

You are usually on your own in all these situations. Being direct and diplomatic is the most recommended way to address these issues. Directness is important, as people are not always skilled in picking up subliminal signals. However, if you are uncomfortable with a direct response or the situation is not too clear, you need to go with what works best for you. Many times a pilot does not feel comfortable speaking up because they often work in a subordinate position (co-pilot or flight engineer) and want to be accepted by their peers and not be perceived as too sensitive or as troublemakers.

The most effective resource in dealing with these encounters is talking with other pilots and hearing about their situations. Some airlines have a committee you can go to called *Professional Standards*. This is a union run group of pilots who talk to both parties involved in a conflict and act as mediators to resolve their differences and help them work better together. In the past, talking with the union or airline management has not been very effective. Again, times are changing and this is improving.

It is important to be aware that these things do happen — maybe they never will to you, maybe they will to your best friend and you can help each other learn more about it. Articles published by ISA and ALPA (Air Line Pilots Association) address these issues more thoroughly.

CHAPTER 9

ONE PILOT'S CAREER PATH

I started flying on a whim when I was 18 and needed a new challenge. I signed up for *Private Pilot Ground School* — whatever that was. I soon found out and after I took my first introductory flight I was hooked. I was living with my parents and working full time, taking my flying lessons after work at an airport near by. It was my big secret until I soloed and just had to tell someone. My parents, however, were not as excited as I was and thought I was wasting my money. But four months after my initial flight I had my license. I sure had a lot to learn, though. I mastered flying *tail draggers* (tail-wheel type airplane) and took a ten hour aerobatics course. I couldn't look up into a bright blue sky without wanting to scribe loops, rolls, and hammer heads in it.

Then someone mentioned A & P (airframe and power-plant mechanics) school and I jumped on it. I was hungry to know all about airplanes. I just wanted to learn the basics and planned to leave after the first semester. Two years later I had my A & P Licenses as well as my commercial and instrument ratings. Then I heard about ATC (Air Traffic Control) school. Everyone close to me discouraged this endeavor; they said it was too hard, that 50% of the people washed out of the four month school, and more during the on the job training. They were right. I did it anyway and finished fourth in my class.

I was an Air Traffic Control Tower Operator for two years and absolutely hated it. I abhorred watching everyone do what I wanted to do — fly airplanes. However, I didn't have the confidence that I could make a living at it. I bought a little airplane and puttered with it, I got my multi-engine rating, and flight instructor ratings — basic, instrument, and multi-engine, but that wasn't enough.

Building flight time to that magic 1200 hours was tough. I flew parachute jumpers, towed gliders & banners, gave airplane rides, flew blood for the red cross & daffodils for the American Cancer Society, and begged pilots to let me fly in the right seat of their twins. Then I quit ATC and started instructing, doing pilot service, and charter work.

When I had almost 1200 hours of flight time, I got a job flying light twin-engine aircraft at night on freight runs, and guess who did all the loading and unloading of the freight? Fifteen long months later I got a job flying turboprops for a regional commuter airline, which I stayed with for two years. The transition from being pilot in command and always in charge to becoming a first officer was a difficult one. When I upgraded to Captain I took all those hard earned lessons and made sure that I wouldn't make the life of my co-pilots as miserable as it had been for me. And that worked well, I had the most wonderful job of my career.

While I was doing all this flying, learning to fly, and side-tracking in other aviation careers, I also worked on a four year degree at night school. After a *mere* nine years, I finally got a Business Aviation degree and had built up enough flight time (4500 hours) to get an airline job.

Getting in the airlines seemed like a full time job: requesting applications and completing and submitting them every month accompanied by the latest updated resume and appropriate letter. I wanted to work for Northwest Airlines so bad

The author standing in the engine of a Boeing 777

that I sent them a letter every week until they responded by asking me to stop writing them. (They never did offer me a job.)

After interviews with three airlines, one hired me. Then another called. I worked for the first one for just under a year and then left. (I was afraid they wouldn't be around for my whole career, and indeed they have since gone bankrupt.) I started at another major, became involved in a pilot strike, was fired for not crossing the picket line, unemployed for five long months, and then re-hired by that same airline. Just over a year later, the airline won a lawsuit and threatened to fire the group I was in, unless we gave up our seniority and started at the bottom, which we did. It wasn't until seven years later when we got our seniority back. The first five years was a troublesome time, partly from the politics, and partly from the difficulties of being a woman in a male-dominated job. It took awhile for me to learn how to deal with bullies and it took awhile for some *good old boys* to learn how to work with people that were different from them.

My aviation career has had some side tracks because there were no resources or role models encouraging me to do what I wanted to do for a living. As an Air Traffic Controller I saw some people who were much older than I who didn't make the sacrifices to achieve the flying career that they really wanted. They were unhappy, angry, and frustrated because they weren't doing what they loved to do.

There are many more resources available now then there were 20 years ago to help keep you on the right track. There are times when you may become discouraged. I was rejected by a commuter airline because they didn't think I could handle their *big* turbo-prop airplanes and now I drive an eighteen wheeler — a Boeing 747-400! Friends and family thought I was chasing smoke and frequently tried to dissuade me because they didn't want to see me fail. But how much bigger a defeat it would have been if I had never tried. You need to realize that many times when people discourage you they are attempting to hold you to their own limitations and if you buy into them you restrict yourself to their definition of life. So go for it!

Any regrets? The knowledge I gained in other aviation fields and every experience I had has helped weave the cloth of who I am today. But yes, I do wish I would have worked more efficiently toward my goal. If I could have taken the leap to try flying for a living earlier and worked continually and diligently on a degree, I would have gotten here quicker. However, I might not have had the maturity that is needed for this job. So whatever route you embrace is probably the best direction for you, as I think it was for me.

AFTERWORD

A note from the Author

Start your flying career today. Take the first step by going to your local airport for a demonstration flight. Call a college you are interested in. Join Aviation Exploring or enroll in private pilot ground school. Phone the military academy you are attracted to and request an information package. Call one of the resources listed in the Appendix now, to help further your career. Each step you take today will get you that much closer to making your dream come true.

Please share this book with your family and friends. The more people who understand what you want to do with your career and how much work it takes to get there, the more help and support you will get. And emotional support is very important, especially if you feel stuck or frustrated. Don't give up. It will all come together.

If you have any input for the author, please write. If you know of organizations that are not mentioned in this book that could be beneficial to further pilot careers, let me know and I will include them in the next edition. You can reach me through Leading Edge Publishing, PO Box 461605, Aurora, CO 80046-1605 or via e-mail: 71322.1370@compuserve.com.

Have a wonderful career *flying the big birds*.

APPENDICES

CAREER OPPORTUNITIES

Aviation Career Counseling

Career counseling to pilots and pilot want-to-be's of all experience levels, given by two airline captains (one regional, one major). They provide current, accurate and impartial advice from professionals who are active in the business. A variety of topics from choosing a flight school, formal education requirements, and financing training, to building flight time, including advanced ratings and type ratings are covered. They also help you with finding aviation employment and discuss how to choose the right airline.

Contact: Aviation Career Counseling, 933 Cheltenham Road, Santa Barbara, CA 93105, 805/687-9493.

Aviation Information Resources, Inc. (AIR Inc.)

This company provides a plethora of information services:

The *Airline Pilot Starter Kit* starts your career from zero hours to getting all certificates and ratings. Over 2000 flight schools are listed (11 recommended), as well as scholarships and grants that are available.

Airline Pilot Career Development System membership incorporates the *Airline Pilot Application Handbook, Airline Pilot Career Decisions Guide, Airline Info & Address Directory, Airline Fleet/Simulator Directory, Airline Career Counseling Services,* and *Airline Pilot Job Monthly Newsletter.* These can all be purchased separately along with an airline resume and cover letter prep service, the *ATP written prep book,* and the *FE written prep book.* Several other books are available: *Airline Pilot Interviews, Airline Pilot Testing Guide, Checklist for Success, Flying in the Guard & Reserve, Military/Airline Transition Guide,* and *Officer Candidate Tests.*

The *Airline Pilot Job Monthly Newsletter* is an informative 12-page newsletter on the changes in the airline industry. It covers industry news and who is hiring, as well as statistics and trends affecting pilot hiring.

The *Airline Info & Address Directory* includes airline addresses of 254 airlines worldwide that hire US pilots, with contacts, benefits, requirements and covers majors, nationals, regionals, and cargo carriers.

Airline Pilot Career Seminar & Job Fair: This is offered several times a year in various parts of the country. Saturday is an all day career seminar imparting information on pilot job market forecasts, job search planning, interviewing techniques, resume & cover letters, employment applications, written and simulator tests, medical exams, and a question-answer session. Career Workshops are available on Friday and Sunday on Cockpit resource management, military/ civilian transition to the airline pilot life, testing/ simulator checks, interviewing, and resumes & applications. A two day prep for the Flight Engineer written test is also available on Sunday and Monday.

Contact: Air Inc., 4002 Riverdale Court, Atlanta, GA 30337-6018; phone 1-800-AIR-APPS or (770) 996-5424; or FAX: 1-800-AIR-FAXS or (770) 996-5547.

J. P. Airline Fleet International

This book is updated and published annually by Buchair US Publications. It is 700 pages of resource information listing 5000 commercial aviation operators — encompassing airlines, commuters, leasing companies, and government agencies, including who to contact. 45,000 airplane listings with current aircraft statistics and information as well as registrations and operators are included. This is a good resource book for researching airlines and corporations when looking for a job.

Contact: Buchair US Publications, PO Box 750515, Forest Hills, NY 11375-0515; phone/FAX (718) 263-8748; or call (212) 606-3790 for 24 hour recording to request a catalogue.

Parc Aviation Limited (PARC)

PARC was owned by Air Lingus for twenty years until 1995, when they became independent. They are the biggest flight crew out-source leasing company in the world, operating in 30 countries with offices in Singapore and Dublin. They currently have 600 flight crews, cabin crews, and engineers (mechanics) on assignment. PARC has worked with 150 airline and aviation companies world wide and is currently working with 40.

A pilot sends in a very detailed resume, fills out an application form, including copies of all licenses and passports, and has a personal or phone interview with PARC. The information is then forwarded to international companies that need pilots to fill a temporary hiring gap of six to twelve months or a contract of three to five years. This is mainly for very experienced pilots who are type rated with 5000 hours. They do get a few requests for low time pilots.

Contact: Parc Aviation Limited, St. John's Court, Swords Road, Santry, Dublin 9, Ireland; phone from the USA 011-353-1-8429-933; FAX 011-353-1-8423-284; E-mail: INTERNET: aviation@parc.ie.; or www.parc.re.

Universal Pilot Application Services, Inc. (UPAS, Inc.)

This is a subscription data base service that retains a qualification summary on a pilot. The information can be updated via mail or computer, through CompuServe. Companies use this information when they have pilot positions available. As of this writing, 47 companies have used this service to search for pilots. These companies vary from one major airline to several regional commuters, jet charter corporations, and private companies. The usual applicant has over 1000 hours of flight time.

Contact: UPAS, 535 Herndon Parkway, PO Box 569, Herndon, VA 22070 or 1-800-PILOT-APPS (1-800-745-6827).

See Also: ORGANIZATIONS AND INFORMATIONAL SOURCES — FAA.

EDUCATION & FLIGHT SCHOOLS

College Catalogs

These are excellent sources of information on the various colleges available and the ones that offer military or flight training combined with a degree. There are numerous catalogs obtainable from your local library and I have listed a few:

Peterson's 4 year Colleges has sections on aviation technology, aviation administration, flight training, and military science. Included is extensive information on the military ROTC program (Reserve Officers Training Corps): *Is it right for you?*, ROTC programs, requirements, and financial scholarships available. For more information contact: College Army ROTC, Gold Quest Center, Attn.: Dept. PG95, PO Box 3279, Warminstr, PA 18974-9872 or 1-800-USA-ROTC.

Lovejoy's College Guide lists colleges that have flying teams and colleges that offer aviation/airway science, aviation administration, and aviation maintenance/systems. ROTC programs for the Army, Air Force, and Navy/Marine can also be found in this section or you can write to each. See: ROTC.

Cass & Birnbaum's Guide to American Colleges lists colleges that offer degree programs in aviation management.

The College Handbook lists military colleges.

ARCO's ROTC College Handbook has more about the ROTC.

Comair Aviation Academy

Comair is a flight training facility that is owned and operated by Comair Airlines, a Delta commuter. They offer all the pilot licenses and certificates from private pilot through flight instructor. You can become one of their flight instructors and built up your flight time to 1000 hours, at which point you are guaranteed an interview with Comair Airlines (97% of those interviewed are offered a job). The Academy is an accredited school with student loans available. Student housing is also available with travel benefits on Comair.

Contact: Comair, 2700 Flight Line Ave., PO Box 1703, Sanford, FL 32772-1703 or phone 1-800-U-CAN-FLY or 1-800-822-6359.

Flight Safety International

Flight Safety operates 150 simulators, 50 of which are used for airline training. Their Academy offers private pilot and career training as well as instructor opportunities as part of its airline career path program. They have 40 learning centers and are an accredited school that offers student loans. Flight Safety also provides business aviation training, airline training, and military and government training.

Contact: Flight Safety Academy, Vero Beach Municipal Airport, PO Box 2708, Vero Beach, FL 32961-2708; phone 1-800-800-1411 or (561) 567-5178; FAX (561) 567-5228; e-mail academy@flightsafety.com; or www.flightsafety.com.

Internship Programs

There are over two dozen aviation-oriented universities that offer flight operations internship programs, with more becoming available every year. If the college you are interested in is not listed, be sure to ask them. The only internship that pays a salary is at UPS (United Parcel Service). Simulator and free flight benefits at the cooperating airlines during the internship are usually available, but the benefits vary. The flight operations internship (usually during the last year of college), normally requires a commercial certificate with instrument and multi-engine ratings, with CFI-A preferred. (Internships are also available in maintenance and management fields.)

American Airlines (AA) has a program with Embry-Riddle Aeronautical University and the University of North Dakota, Grand Forks, ND.

Delta Air Lines (DAL) works with: Embry-Riddle Aeronautical University; Louisiana Tech University, Ruston, LA; Southern Illinois University, Carbondale, IL; and Utah State University, Logan, UT.

Federal Express (Fed EX) has programs with: Embry-Riddle; Louisiana Tech University, Ruston, LA; and Middle Tennessee State University, Murfreesboro, TN.

Northwest Orient Airlines (NWA) works with: Mankato State University, Mankato, MN; St. Cloud State, St. Cloud, MN; and University of North Dakota, Grand Forks, ND.

Trans World Airlines (TWA) is involved with: Central Missouri State University, Warrensburg, MO; Dowling College, NY; Embry-Riddle Aeronautical University; Ohio University, Athens, OH; Ohio State University, Columbus, OH; Parks College of St. Louis University; and Southern Illinois University, Carbondale, IL.

United Airlines (UAL) has programs with: Arizona State University, Tempe, AZ; Central Missouri State University, Warrensburg, MO; Daniel Webster College, Nashua, NH; Delaware State University, Dover, DE; Embry-Riddle Aeronautical University, Daytona Beach, FL and Prescott, AZ; Florida Institute of Technology, Melbourne, FL; Kent State University, Kent, OH; Louisiana Tech University, Ruston, LA; Metropolitan State College, Denver, CO; Middle Tennessee State University, Murfreesboro, TN; Ohio State University, Columbus, OH; Ohio University, Athens, OH; Parks College, Cahokia, IL; Purdue University, West Lafayette, IN; San Jose State University, San Jose, CA; Southern Illinois University,

Carbondale, IL; University of Illinois, Champaign-Urbana, IL; University of North Dakota, Grand Forks, ND; Utah State University, Logan, UT; and Western Michigan University, Kalamazoo, MI.

United Parcel Service (UPS) works with: Middle Tennessee State University, Murfreesboro, TN; Purdue University, West Lafayette, IN; and Southern Illinois University, Carbondale, IL.

US Air has internship programs with: Embry-Riddle Aeronautical University, Daytona Beach, FL; Ohio State University, Columbus, OH; Ohio University, Athens, OH; and Purdue University, West Lafayette, IN.

Professional Instrument Courses, Inc. (PIC Services, Inc.)

PIC gives a 10 day course for the instrument rating at the student's location, anywhere in the US. They travel to the student, set up a portable simulator in your house, and give simulator and flight training (in the student's airplane). They also offer a manual called *The Instrument Flight Training Manual.*

If you would like to become one of their instructors, you need a minimum of 3000 hours total time and CFII experience.

Contact: PIC Inc., Aviation Center, 30 Plains Road, Essex, CT 06426 or phone 1-800-425-9437.

University Aviation Association (UAA)

UAA's goal is to encourage and promote the highest standards in aviation education in college. They have aviation experts available for consultation and speaking engagements, foster information exchange among aviation institutions, sponsor intercollegiate flying through the NIFA (National Intercollegiate Flying Association) and support teacher education.

They offer a plethora of publications to members and non-members. *Collegiate Aviation Guide* is a must-have directory of over 280 colleges and universities that have aviation programs. This catalog includes admission requirements, degrees offered, tuition, accreditation, aviation opportunities and internships, placement services, scholarships, cost of flight education, and more. (Also available through Sporty's Pilot Shop.)

Collegiate Aviation Scholarship Listing is a listing of publicly available information concerning collegiate aviation scholarships. Included are scholarships available from various organizations, amounts, deadlines and other useful information. There are also loan programs listed that are available to aviation students.

Aviation Publications Directory is a listing of aviation texts, reference books and audio visual materials. *Collegiate Aviation Training Aircraft and Flight Training Devices* includes information on aviation training aircraft and simulators and costs of ratings and degrees from 119 colleges and universities.

Contact: UAA, 3410 Skyway Drive, Auburn, Alabama 36830 or (334) 844-2434.

See Also: CAREER OPPORTUNITIES — Aviation Career Counseling and AIR Inc.; ORGANIZATIONS AND INFORMATIONAL SOURCES — AOPA, ALPA, and OBAP; INTERVIEWING RESOURCES — Arnautical; and WOMEN'S ORGANIZATIONS.

INTERVIEWING RESOURCES

Airline Pilot Employment Advisors (APEA)

This company helps you get prepared for your airline interview. The owner, Irv Jasinski has ten years of experience as a manager of employment and pilot recruitment for the Flying Tiger Line (which has since merged with Fed Ex). He has interviewed and selected hundreds of pilots, as well as taught interviewing techniques at universities and pilot candidate seminars at flight schools. Mr. Jasinski will review your resume and conduct a mock interview geared to the airline with whom you have your interview. He has also written a book called *Airline Pilot Interviews — How you can succeed in getting hired,* which provides techniques and information to guide you in the interview.

Contact: APEA, PO Box 271409, Escondido, CA 92027 or phone (619) 489-9419.

Airline Pilot Testing Guide

By Clark St. John. This book provides sample aptitude and personality tests to help you prepare for the tests given by the airlines. Contact: Your local bookstore or AIR Inc.

Arnautical Inc.

Arnautical was founded in 1973 by a United Airlines pilot and is currently owned and run by two UAL pilots. They offer a pre-hire training program that consists of simulator training and interview preparation. The simulator training is done in a jet speed FRASCA simulator comparable to the one used by United Airlines employment screening personnel, using similar flight profiles as in the interview process. They also use United Airlines Simulators for warm up for simulator checks and interviewing with other airlines.

The interview preparation reviews your application, covers recommended interview techniques along with critique and feedback to your responses. They also offer a video taping option. Attitude, body language, and expectations of the interviewers will also be covered.

Arnautical cooperates with United son's and daughter's program and also offers type ratings in the Boeing 727, 737, 757/767, 777, and 747-400.

Contact: Arnautical, Hanger 9, Box B-5, 7375 South Peoria Street, Englewood, CO 80112; phone 1-800-333-3JET or (303) 649-1002; or FAX (303) 649-9558.

Cage Consulting, Inc.

This company provides pilot career preparation services to help you get a job with major and commuter airlines, as well as corporate pilot positions. They offer interview preparation consultation, application and resume reviewing, and career counseling. A military transition package is available to help a pilot learn what to expect during a civilian job search.

An invaluable tool available for pilots of all experience levels is book written by Cheryl Cage titled: *Checklist for Success: A pilot's Guide to the Successful Airline Interview*. This book has information on getting an interview, steps to a successful interview, physical and paperwork presentations, common concerns for the applicant, advice from airline pilots, and sample interview questions. A workbook is incorporated with checklists of things to do before, during and after the interview, along with sample resume and cover letters.

Contact: Cage Consulting, PO Box 460327, Aurora CO 80046-0327 or 7208 South Tucson Way, Suite 120, Englewood, CO 80112, phone (303) 799-1991, FAX: (303)799-1998.

Sweaty Palms — The Neglected Art of Being Interviewed

By H. Anthony Medley. This is a book for gaining general interviewing knowledge and has been recommended by some airline pilots. It covers all the basics: preparation, types of interviews, the interview, dress, confidence, nervousness, questions and answers, etc. Checklists at the end of each chapter are included along with commonly asked questions and queries to check your references. Contact: Your local bookstore.

See Also: CAREER OPPORTUNITIES — AIR Inc.

MILITARY CONTACTS

Military

If you are interested in going the military route, thoroughly check out each service to find one right for you.

For requirements and admission applications to the academies contact: US Air Force Academy, Colorado Springs, CO 80840 or 1-800-443-3864. For counseling assistance write to the Admissions office, HQ USAF/RRS, 2304 Cadet Drive, Suite 200, USAF Academy, Colorado 80840-5025. To schedule a visit, call (719) 333-2233, allow about ten days lead time.

Contact the US Military Academy (Army), West Point, NY 10996 or (914) 938-4041.

Contact the US Naval Academy (Navy and Marine Corps), 117 Decatur Road, Annapolis, MD 21402-5018 or 1-800-638-9156.

Contact the US Coast Guard Academy, New London, CT.

ARCO Officer Candidate Tests is a must read book before taking any OTS/OCS written or physical exams. This book covers career opportunities and requirements, requirements to earning a commission in each service, and the military tests. Preparation and studying for tests, practice exercises, and occupational descriptions are also included. Check in your bookstore or library for the latest edition. Air, Inc. also has the book available.

Reserve Officer Training Corps. (ROTC)

For requirements and admission applications contact: Army ROTC, Headquarters Cadet Command, Fort Monroe, VA, 23651-5000; Navy-Marine Corps ROTC, 801 North Randolph Street, Arlington, VA 22203-9933 or call 1-800-NAV-ROTC; and HQ Air Force ROTC Recruiting Division, 551 E. Maxwell Blvd., Maxwell Air Force Base, AL 36112-6106.

See Also: EDUCATION & FLIGHT SCHOOLS — College Catalogs; ORGANIZATIONS AND INFORMATIONAL SOURCES — CAP; and WOMEN'S ORGANIZATIONS — WMA.

ORGANIZATIONS AND INFORMATIONAL SOURCES

Aircraft Owners and Pilots Association (AOPA)

AOPA represents more than 300,000 general aviation aircraft owners and pilots across the US and offers a wealth of educational resources to teachers, schools and AOPA members. Education materials available are: A Teacher's Guide to Aviation, APPLE (AOPA aviation education program) Classroom Kit, ABC's of Aviation (aviation-to-English dictionary), Careers in Aviation, Aviation Fact Card, and AOPA Pilot Magazine. They also have a sweepstakes for a Cessna 182.

AOPA's Flight Fund is a loan program available to AOPA members. Call 1-800-441-7048 ext. 65932.

Contact: AOPA, 421 Aviation Way, Frederick, MD 21701 or phone 1-800-638-3101, (301) 695-2000 or FAX (301) 695-2375.

Air Line Pilots Association (ALPA)

ALPA represents 42,000 airline pilots at 37 airlines, promoting better working conditions, wages, safety, technology, and legislation. They participate in aviation education through their Education Committee and the Pilot Information Program (PIP). PIP is an organization designed for anyone interested in becoming a pilot. Members receive information on becoming a pilot and what it's like to be a pilot. They receive the ALPA magazine, a quarterly newsletter, a copy of *Flying the Line* (a history of airline flying), and a discount to Air Inc. ALPA also participates in NIFA (National Intercollegiate Flying Association) through $500 and $1000 awards. Scholarships are available for children of deceased or medically retired ALPA pilots.

Contact: Don Skiados, ALPA, 1625 Massachusetts Avenue NW, Washington, DC 20036; phone (202) 797-4060; or FAX (202) 797-4052.

Aviation Exploring

This is a division of the Boy Scouts of America that is an aviation based program open to young men and women ages 14 through 20. Explorers plan and operate their own Explorer post with the guidance of an adult advisor. You may take orientation flights in military transports, helicopters, gliders, or single engine general aviation aircraft; trips to Air Force bases, aviation museums, airshows, or FAA facilities; preflight an aircraft or take pilot training ground school. The Explorer posts work with the local FBO (Fixed Base Operator or flight school), the FAA (Federal Aviation Administration), the EAA (Experimental Aircraft Association), and some major airlines (United Airlines in Denver and San Francisco, American Airlines in Chicago and Dallas, Delta Airlines in Atlanta, etc.).

For example, the Denver post goes on outings to an FBO, Denver International Air Traffic Control Tower, Fire and Rescue, United ramp and customer services, United Operations (pilot flight planning and briefing), United's Maintenance Base (exploring the aircraft and cockpit), and United's Training Center (touring the facility, going through the evacuation simulator, aircraft mock-ups, and flying the aircraft flight simulator.)

Contact: Boy Scouts of America, 1325 West Walnut Hill Lane, PO Box 152079, Irving, Texas 75015-2079 or (214) 580-2000.

Civil Air Patrol (CAP)

The CAP began before WW II as a not-for-profit volunteer civilian auxiliary of the US Air Force. It has grown to more than 50,000 active members. Its primary missions are aerospace education, emergency services, and Cadet programs. The CAP sponsors 200 workshops in colleges and universities across the nation. Their emergency services include search and rescue, disaster relief, humanitarian services, and counter-drug operations. The Cadet program's primary function is to develop the potential of young people, age 13 to 21, through physical fitness, leadership training, and aerospace education. They have summer camps where they do training, along with flight orientation in their fleet of more than 530 light aircraft.

Contact: CAP, National Headquarters, 105 South Handles Street, Bldg. 714, Maxwell AFB, AL 36112-6332; phone 1-800-FLY-2338; INTERNET:http://www.cap.af.mil; or look up the local chapter in your phone book.

Experimental Aircraft Association (EAA)

EAA's mission is to serve all of aviation by fostering and encouraging participation in flying. It is for pilots, designers, and builders and anyone who enjoys aviation. The EAA also has a museum and Boeing library at its headquarters.

Membership includes a subscription to *Sport Aviation,* the Oshkosh convention, and an opportunity to participate in a local chapter. (See Young Eagles). There are also three divisions within EAA for members with special interests. The antique/classic division focuses on vintage airplanes. The International Aerobatic Club (IAC) division is for members to learn about or compete in aerobatics. EAA warbirds of America is dedicated to preserving ex-military aircraft.

EAA Oshkosh is a famous, week long annual fly-in convention in Oshkosh, WI. Aviation enthusiasts from all over the world come to participate in daily air shows, educational forums, and hands-on workshops.

Contact: EAA, PO Box 3086, Oshkosh, WI 54903-3086; phone 1-800-843-3612; or FAX (414) 426-6761. EAA web page is: http://www.eaa.org.

Federal Aviation Administration (FAA)

The FAA has free brochures available on each major job category in its aviation career series. Some examples are an overview brochure entitled *Your Career in Aviation: The Sky's the Limit,* as well as *Pilots & Flight Engineers* and *Women in Aviation.* Six other booklets are avaiable about additional aviation careers: (flight attendants, non-flying careers, aircraft manufacturing, aviation maintenance and avionics, airport and government careers).

Send a self-addressed mailing label with your request to: Superintendent of Documents, Retail Distribution Division, Consigned Branch, 8610 Cherry Lane, Laurel, MD 20707.

The FAA also has a phone number with a recorded message of the aviation careers that are open or available at the FAA: air traffic controller (ATC), aviation safety inspector, air space systems inspector, and flight test pilot. A general description of each career is provided, with the minimum qualifications required. Information packets can be requested on specific jobs that are available. Contact the Aviation Careers Unit in Oklahoma City at (405) 954-4657.

4-H Youth Programs

This organization is dedicated to developing new opportunities for youth and society by being involved in aviation and space education with exciting programs such as 4-H Missions in Space at Space Camp in Huntsville, Alabama. (Space Camp is also available at NASA's Kennedy space Center in Florida and NASA's Ames Research Center in Mountain View, California.) This partnership provides opportunities for young people to participate in special three, six or eight day versions of the Space Academy level one program. Several sessions are conducted each year for young people in the 4th grade or higher.

Space Academy, level one is open for grades 6 through 8 and level two for grades 9 through 12 at the Alabama Campus. Aviation Challenge is another course that introduces you to the experience of military jet pilot training, starting with the fundamentals of flying, then progressing through sophisticated simulator missions. Basic is offered to grades 7 through 9 and intermediate for grades 9 through 12. Parent-child space camp is available, as well as programs for adults (Space Academy and Aviation Challenge). Call the group reservation's manager at 1-800-63-SPACE.

4-H also works with the EAA Young Eagles program and offers a publication called *Skylights*, that addresses some of the current needs in aerospace education. The National 4-H Council has a newsletter and its individual state groups conduct camps and programs related to aerospace.

Contact: Dr. Tony Cook, National Project Coordinator, 4-H Aerospace Education Programs, 211 Duncan Hall — ACES, Auburn University, AL 36849-5620; phone (205) 844-2233; or FAX (205) 844-9650.

National Coalition for Aviation Education (NCAE) — A Guide to Aviation Education Resources

NCAE represents industry and labor united to promote aviation education activities and resources, increase public understanding of the importance of aviation, and support educational initiatives. Their guide lists a plethora of organizations that offer career information, education, scholarships, and youth programs. They also offer information on careers in helicopters, the soaring society (gliders/sailplanes), agricultural aviation (cropdusting), and non-flying aviation

careers such as aviation business, airports, aircraft maintenance and electronics.

Contact: NCAE, PO Box 28086, Washington, DC 20038.

Opportunity Skyway

This group was founded in 1990 and is a hands-on, experi-
ential drop-out prevention and career development program.
It focuses on preparing minority and disadvantaged youngsters for a broad range of careers in aeronautics and transportation. Programs are available in elementary school,
middle school and high school. They also help academically
qualified students who lack financial resources to move on to
two-year technical schools and four-year degree programs.
Opportunity Skyway Clubs organize orientation flights, tours
of aeronautical facilities, schedule speakers, hold career days,
and prepare members for private pilot ground school.

Contact: Deszerrai Shannon, Opportunity Skyway, 6709
Cpl. Frank S. Scott Drive, College Park, MD 20740; phone
(301) 864-0673; or FAX (310) 864-0849.

Organization of Black Airline Pilots (OBAP)

The goals of OBAP are to motivate youth to become edu-
cationally prepared for life, to increase African-American
participation in aviation, to encourage networking among eth-
nic minority pilots, and to assist these pilots with special
needs or concerns.

Airlines first began hiring black pilots in 1963, but there
are still less than 1% of African-Americans in the industry today. OBAP began in 1976 and has established a scholarship
fund to carry out a variety of philanthropic acts. One project
sponsors high school students to participate in the NAI
Summer Flight Academy in Tuskegee, Alabama. There they
partake in two weeks of intense aviation education, discipline,
and acquire ten hours of flight training. OBAP also provides
professional pilot development and career guidance for

aspiring airline pilots by offering fellowships and type rating scholarships. There are several different memberships available and they are open to everyone.

Contact: OBAP, c/o Stanley McWilliams, PO Box 43952, Los Angeles, CA 90043; OBAP, PO Box 50666, Phoenix, AZ 85076-0666; or call 1-800-JET-OBAP.

Space Camp

See 4-H Youth Programs for information and details.

Young Eagles Program

This program started in 1992 and is sponsored by the Experimental Aircraft Association (EAA). The objectives are to encourage young people to become interested in flying, raise awareness of available aviation careers, and promote an understanding of what is required to become a pilot. Eagle Flight membership is open to people age 8 to 17. As a member you receive a demonstration flight, an issue of *Sport Aviation For Kids* magazine, and your name listed in the world's largest logbook. You also receive information on aviation organizations and activities in your area and information on scholarship programs administered by the EAA.

Contact: The Young Eagles Office, PO Box 2683, Oshkosh, WI 54903-2683 or call (414) 426-4831. Information is also available on the web at http://www.eaa.org.

See Also: CAREER OPPORTUNITIES — AIR Inc. and WOMEN'S ORGANIZATIONS.

Scholarships

National Air Transportation Association (NATA) & National Air Transportation Foundation (NATF)

NATA is a public policy group that represents thousands of aviation businesses before Congress and Federal agencies. They publish several monthly and quarterly newsletters for company members that are engaged in the business of aviation. The research and educational arm of NATA is the National Air Transportation Foundation (NATF).

NATF has established the Pioneers of Flight Scholarship Program, managed by Citizens' Scholarship Foundation of America, Inc. (CSFA). CSFA screens all scholarship applications, while NAFT makes the final selection.

Applicants for the Pioneers of Flight Scholarship must be nominated by a NATA member, be a college student in their sophomore or junior year, and demonstrate an interest in pursing a career in General Aviation. An application must be filled out and submitted with a grade transcript by November 22. Up to four, $2500 awards are granted each year for full-time study and are renewable once if a GPA of 2.5 is maintained.

Contact: Pioneers of Flight Scholarship Program, Citizens' Scholarship Foundation of America, Inc., 1505 Riverview Road, PO Box 297, St. Peter, MN 56082 or phone (507) 931-1682.

NATF also sponsors the John E. Godwin Memorial Scholarship. Screening of applicants is done by the officers and directors of the National Association of Flight Instructors, with the final selection made by NATF. To be eligible you must be at least 18 years old, be nominated by a member of NATA, possess a Student Pilot Certificate with a third class medical (and able to qualify for a second class), demonstrate a commitment to General Aviation, and it is recommended that you be a member of the Civil Air Patrol (CAP). Applications must be submitted by November 15. $2500 is awarded annually for the purpose of flight training for any pilot certificate and/or flight rating.

Contact: John E. Godwin, Jr. Memorial Scholarship Fund, National Air Transportation Foundation, 4226 King Street, Alexandria, VA 22302, phone (703) 845-9000, or FAX (703) 845-8176.

See Also: EDUCATION & FLIGHT SCHOOLS — UAA; ORGANIZATIONS & INFORMATIONAL SOURCES — ALPA, NCAE, and OBAP; TRAINING PRODUCTS — Sporty's Pilot Shop; and WOMEN'S ORGANIZATIONS.

Training Products

Aviation Supplies & Academics, Inc. (ASA)

ASA carries a variety of training manuals for pilot certificates and ratings. They also publish a *FAR/AIM* book that includes all the Federal Aviation Regulations and the Aeronautical Information Manual (which is a guide that provides a plethora of basic flight information, emergency procedures, safety of flight, air traffic control procedures, and a pilot/ controller glossary). Most aviation book stores or flight schools/FBO's (Fixed base operators) carry this book or you can contact them directly.

Contact: ASA, 7005 132nd Place SE, Newcastle, WA 98059-3153 or phone 1-800-ASA-2FLY (1-800-272-2359).

Federal Aviation Regulations (FARs)

Be sure to check each of the FARs for specifics and changes. FAR 61 gives details on Pilot certifications and ratings. FAR 67 describes the medical standards for each class of medical certificate. Check for disqualifying conditions if you are not in perfect health. For example, diabetes requiring insulin or medication is disqualifying, as well as epilepsy, heart disease, disturbance of equilibrium, and substance abuse.

FAR 91 has the general operating and flight rules. FAR 135 carries the air taxi operations. FAR 141 discusses flight schools.

FAR books are published by ASA and Jeppesen and are available from them directly, by catalogue, or at your local aviation book store.

Jeppesen Sanderson, Inc.

Jeppesen carries a variety of training manuals for pilot certificates and ratings, as well as maps and approach chart subscriptions. They also publish books covering all the applicable FARs and a *FAR/AIM* book. Most aviation book stores or flight schools/FBO's (Fixed base operators) carry this book or you can contact them directly.

Contact: Jeppesen Sanderson, Inc., Attn.: Sales and Service, 55 Inverness Drive East, Englewood, CO 80112-5498.

Jet Stream Catalog

Jet Stream offers flight planners, pilot & cockpit accessories, pilot training videos & books, software, and simulator technology.

Contact: Jet Stream Catalog, 3355 NE Cornell Road, Hillsboro, OR 97124-6380; phone 1-800-470-2359; or FAX 1-800-470-0434.

King Schools

King offers a variety of ground school courses and exam reviews in both video and computer format. They also have a sweepstakes for a Mooney airplane.

Contact: King Schools, 3840 Calle Fortunada, San Diego, CA 92123; phone 1-800-854-1001 or (619) 541-2200; or FAX (619) 541-2201.

Magazines

Flight Training Magazine is a monthly proficiency and career magazine. Periodically the magazine will list an extensive Flight School Directory. Flight Training and the National Air Transportation Association have a pamphlet available that provides a checklist for helping you select a flight school. If you hold a current FAA student pilot certificate you can receive a six month subscription free. Contact: Flight Training Magazine, 405 Main Street, Parkville, MO 64152; phone (816) 741-5151; or FAX (815) 741-6458.

Flying, Plane & Pilot, and **Private Pilot** magazines contain articles that are both educational and informative as well advertise numerous companies that offer training product and flight training schools. Contact your local book store.

Pilot Training Publications Co.

This is a company that offers a free catalogue of flight training materials available for all pilot certificates. It also sells ICAO (International Civil Aviation Organization) publications. Some of the subjects that its books cover are: agricultural pilot, ATP, aviation law, commercial pilot, flight training and career guides, instrument rating, meteorology, multi-engine rating, private pilot, seaplane rating, and written test guides. Many of the books offered are listed in the CompuServe flight training/careers library on AVSIG in the file STUDY.TXT.

Contact: Pilot Training Publications Co., PO Box 394, Mountain View, CA 94042-0394 or phone (415) 962-1097.

Sporty's Pilot Shop

Sporty's is a very large catalog pilot shop. It carries flight training and aviation education materials (books, videos, charts and chart subscriptions) as well as gifts and aviation stuff to make you look like a really cool pilot. Sporty's also offers some wonderful aviation scholarships and has a yearly drawing for a free Cessna Skyhawk airplane.

Sporty's awards two aviation scholarships to full-time high school or college students. The scholarships each pay up to $15,000 to be used over a two-year period for pilot certificates and ratings. To qualify, you must be enrolled in a high school college prep course or a college. You must submit transcripts as well as scores on either the ACT or SAT tests. An essay on aviation is required with two recommendation letters. For one of the scholarships the selection committee may give preference to a student interested or enrolled in the University of Cincinnati, Clermont College Professional Pilot Technology Program. The deadline is January 15.

Contact: Sporty's Aviation Scholarship Program, PO Box 44327, Cincinnati, OH 45244 or call 1-800-LIFTOFF (1-800-543-8633).

Women's Organizations

International Society of Women Airline Pilots (ISA+21)

ISA started as the International Social Affiliation of Women Airline Pilots in 1978. Twenty-one women pilots from ten US airlines gathered together for camaraderie and to discuss the difficulties of being a female in a male-dominated environment. It has grown to an organization of over 500 members worldwide from 32 countries and 92 airlines. ISA members assist aspiring women pilots entering the industry through the ISA speakers and information bank (speaking at local schools, colleges, civic clubs, and community gatherings), networking, service projects, and scholarships.

Scholarships are available for advanced pilot ratings and type ratings. The Fiorenza DeBernardi Merit Award Scholarship is open to pilots who have not yet attained their ATP (Air Transport Pilot) or FE (Flight Engineer) ratings. The Holly Mullins Memorial Scholarship is available for single mothers. Each one requires a minimum of 350 hours of flight time. Career scholarships have been donated by several different airlines and are available for Flight Engineer and Type Ratings. These require a minimum of 750 flight hours, a current First Class Medical, and a Commercial Pilot Certificate with an Instrument Rating. Additionally 1000 hours and a current FE written are required for a Flight Engineer Scholarship. An ATP and FE written are required for the Type Rating Scholarship. Scholarship deadlines are April 1.

Membership is available to all women pilots who are employed as flight crew members with a FAR Part 121 or equivalent air carrier that operates at least one aircraft with a gross weight of 90,000 pounds or more.

Contact: ISA, 2250 East Tropicana Avenue, Suite 19-395, Las Vegas, Nevada, 89119-6541.

The Ninety-Nines, Inc. (the 99's)

An international women pilot organization started in 1929 by 99 female pilots with Amelia Earhart as the first president. The 99's is primarily educational and philanthropic. Their mission is to promote world fellowship through flight, preserve the unique history of women in aviation, and provide networking and scholarship opportunities. They sponsor educational programs such as aerospace education workshops for teachers, airport tours for school children, and aviation talks to service clubs. The 99's also offer co-pilot clinics for airline passengers, flight instructor revalidation courses, and pilot safely programs. They sponsor the National Intercollegiate Flying Association and the US Precision Flight Team.

The 99's offer a variety of scholarships. Several Amelia Earhart Memorial Scholarships for advanced flight training are awarded each year. An Amelia Earhart Research Scholar Grant is available, as well as the 99's Award of Merit and the Marion Barnick Memorial Scholarship. The Katherine B. Wright Memorial Trophy, honoring the sister of Wilbur and Orville Wright is also available.

A bi-monthly magazine is included with a membership. This is a group where you can make friends with other female aviators, help the community with your flying (fly blood for the Red Cross or daffodils for the American Cancer Society), and have fun.

Contact: The Ninety-Nines, Inc., Box 965, 7100 Terminal Drive, Oklahoma City, OK 73159; phone (405) 685-7969; or FAX (405) 685-7985.

The Whirly-Girls, Inc.

Whirly-Girls was formed in 1955 to join the twelve licensed women helicopter pilots in France, Germany, and the USA. Today there are over 1000 members in 29 countries. The Whirly-Girls are dedicated to advancing professionalism in helicopters, while providing women helicopter pilots a forum for the exchange of information and opportunities. There are several memberships available for both men and women.

Contact: Jean Tinsley, Whirly-Girls Inc., PO Box 7446, Menlo Park, CA 94026; phone (415) 462-1441; or e-mail Whirlygrls@AOL.COM.

The Whirly-Girls provide four scholarships to women pilots to obtain flight ratings. The Whirly-Girls Helicopter flight training scholarship assists a female who is currently a fixed-wing, glider, or balloon pilot to add a helicopter rating ($4500). The Doris Mullen Scholarship provides funds to a member for advanced ratings ($4500). The Bell Helicopter Scholarship is for a member for a turbine transition. The Pritchard Corporate Air Service Lend-a-hand Scholarship is for a licensed female pilot to obtain a commercial helicopter rating and CFI. The training is one year, followed by six months of employment as a flight instructor for Pritchard Air. Scholarship deadline is November 15.

Contact: Charlotte Kelley, WG #21, 207 W. Clarendon, Apt. 10-D, Phoenix AZ 85013; phone (602) 263-0190; or FAX (602) 264-5812.

Women in Aviation, International (WAI)

WAI was established to encourage women to seek opportunities in aviation by providing resources to assist women. WAI offers educational outreach programs to educators, aviation industry members, and young people. The quarterly publication includes an aviation networking section where you can find a variety of contacts, from information on pilot career opportunities and education, to aircraft mechanics and air traffic control.

WAI has served as an umbrella organization for specialized women's aviation groups: Women Military Aviators, Inc., Women Air Force Service Pilots, and others. They also have a web site on the internet with about ten pages on schools and other career resources at: http: //www. aircruise.com/aca/wia.

Annually, WAI puts on the International Women in Aviation Conference, which is a venue for women and men to explore opportunities in aviation. Forums include a variety of topics to help you stay abreast of current trends and issues in aviation. A special emphasis is on career advancement and development, as well as technical information and safety issues.

Membership is open to women and men from all segments of the aviation industry: general, corporate, commercial, and military, as well as aviation professionals and students. Membership includes: the annual international conference, on-line service through CompuServe (WIAonline), and *Women in Aviation, The Publication*. Government and industry representation, educational outreach programs, and a networking base for career and personal development are also a part of the membership.

Contact: Dr. Peggy Baty, WAI, Inc., PO Box 188, 1 Chamber Plaza, Suite A, Dayton, OH 45402; phone (513) 225-9440; or FAX (513) 225-9455.

Women Military Aviators, Inc. (WMA)

It wasn't until the early 1970's that women were allowed to officially enter military aviation. In 1973 the Navy opened up pilot training to women. The Army and Coast Guard soon followed and in 1976 the Air Force sanctioned pilot training for women. The Aviation Combat Exclusion Laws were repealed in 1991 and with a subsequent policy change in 1993 women are now allowed to fly as crew members in all military aircraft (including the Marines) except for Special Operations helicopters.

WMA was formed in 1978 by the Women Air Force Service Pilots (WASP) of World War II for the present-day military women. It is a non-profit organization formed to promote and preserve the historic, educational, and literary role of women serving as military aviators. Their membership numbers over 650 and includes WASP, Air Force, Army, Navy, Coast Guard, Marines, and Allied Forces. All women military aviators are able to become members, including active duty and reserve, officer and enlisted, and former crew members.

WMA publishes a quarterly newsletter and holds biennial conferences. A $2500 scholarship is awarded annually, and can be used for a private pilot license. Each year the scholarship is named to honor a deceased woman military aviator.

Contact: WMA, Inc., PO Box 46819, Washington, DC 20050-4817.

Zonta International Foundation

This is a worldwide service organization of 36,000 executives in business and professions working together to advance the status of women. (Amelia Earhart was a member.) Each year Zonta awards $6000 in annual grants to women for graduate studies. Fellowships are open to women of any nationality. Grants may be used in any institution offering fully accredited graduate courses and degrees in aerospace related sciences and engineering. To apply, a woman must have at least a BS in a qualifying area of science or engineering, a high academic record, and have completed one year of graduate school in a program related to aerospace-related sciences. Applications are due November 1 of each year.

Contact: Zonta International Foundation, 557 West Randolph Street, Chicago, IL 60661-2204; phone (312) 930-5848; or FAX (312) 930-0951.

ORDER FORM

To order books directly from the publisher, please send $14.95 plus $2.00 for postage and handling for each book. (Colorado residents add $1.13 sales tax.)

Please Print or Type:

Name_____

Street_____

City_____State_____Zip_____

Send to:

Leading Edge Publishing
PO Box 461605
Aurora, CO 80046-1605